To the hearts that have loved and lost,
To those who found strength in their scars,
And to anyone still searching for closure.

This book is for the dreamers who dared to love deeply,
the broken who refused to stay shattered,
and the poets who turn pain into art.

May you find solace in these words,
and may you always remember,
healing begins within.

FALL IN LOVE: TO BREAK YOUR OWN HEART

SURAJ DAS

Contents

Contents

Foreword

Love is a journey, not always linear, and often not easy. It is a kaleidoscope of emotions—joy, longing, heartbreak, and healing. In this book, I have tried to capture the essence of that journey, drawn from the deepest corners of my heart.

Fall in Love: To Break Your Own Heart is not just a story; it is a reflection of the vulnerability, resilience, and growth that love brings into our lives. Through Suraj's experiences, I hope to convey the beauty of loving wholeheartedly, the pain of letting go, and the strength required to start anew.

This book is as much about finding love as it is about losing it—and rediscovering yourself in the process. It's about how we weave our stories through connection, how we grow through the pain, and how we ultimately rise stronger.

Every poem within these pages is a piece of that emotional tapestry—a glimpse into the raw, unfiltered moments that shape us. It is my hope that these words resonate with you, that you see a bit of your own story in them, and that they remind you: even in heartbreak, there is beauty, and even in endings, there are new beginnings.

Thank you for embarking on this journey with me.

With gratitude and hope,

Suraj Das

Preface

Love is often celebrated as the most beautiful emotion one can experience, but it also holds the power to break us in ways we never imagined. This book was born from that duality—a love so profound it changed me, and a heartbreak so devastating it reshaped me.

Fall in Love: To Break Your Own Heart is a deeply personal narrative, inspired by the complexities of relationships, the weight of unspoken emotions, and the struggles of moving on. It is a story about Suraj, a dreamer who loved with all his heart, and Parvati, a free spirit who brought both joy and pain into his life.

This book is not just about their journey together but also about the aftermath of love—the messy, painful, and transformative path of healing. It explores the questions we all face: How do you let go of someone who once meant everything to you? How do you rebuild yourself when your heart feels shattered?

Through every chapter, I have tried to weave moments of joy, heartbreak, and reflection, accompanied by poems that serve as windows into the emotions that words often fail to capture.

This is not a guide to love, nor a manual for heartbreak. It is simply a story—a story of falling, breaking, and rising again. If you have ever loved deeply, lost painfully, or found yourself at a crossroads in the aftermath, this book is for you.

Thank you for taking the time to step into this world, and I hope you find pieces of yourself within these pages.

Acknowledgements

Writing Fall in Love: To Break Your Own Heart has been an emotional and transformative journey, one that I could not have completed without the support of so many incredible beings.

First and foremost, I want to thank my family for their unwavering belief in me. Your encouragement gave me the strength to pour my heart onto these pages, even when it wasn't easy.

To my friends, who listened patiently to countless drafts, ideas, and moments of doubt—thank you for being my sounding boards and my safe havens. Your guidance and honesty were invaluable in shaping this story.

A very special thank you to my pet, Barfi, whose presence brought warmth and light into even my darkest days. Barfi, you stayed with me every single day, reminding me that love can be pure, unconditional, and healing. You made me believe in love in its truest form, and for that, I am endlessly grateful.

To the heartbreaks and the healing that inspired this book: while the pain was difficult to bear, it taught me lessons I never knew I needed. This book wouldn't exist without those experiences, and for that, I am grateful.

To my readers, who will soon hold this book in their hands—thank you for allowing me to share this story with you. Your time and connection to these words mean the world to me. I hope you find comfort, understanding, and perhaps a piece of your own story reflected here.

Lastly, to love itself: for teaching me that even in its most painful forms, it holds the power to transform us into something stronger, wiser, and more beautiful than before.

Prologue

Love has a way of sneaking up on you—softly, unexpectedly, and with an intensity that takes your breath away. It wraps you in its embrace, makes you believe in forever, and gives you a reason to dream. But love, too, can shatter you. It can leave you stranded, questioning everything you thought you knew about yourself and the world.

This is not just a story about love; it's a story about what happens when love breaks. It's about the beauty of first kisses and the ache of final goodbyes. It's about the promises that fade, the scars that linger, and the people who leave their marks on our hearts, even as they walk away.

In the heart of this story is Suraj, a dreamer who believed that love could conquer all, and Parvati, a vibrant spirit who brought color into his life, only to take it away. Their journey is one of passion, heartbreak, and self-discovery—a journey many of us have walked at some point in our lives.

But this isn't just about heartbreak. It's about the resilience of the human spirit. It's about how we pick up the pieces, learn to trust again, and find love where we least expect it. Sometimes, the most meaningful love stories are the ones we write for ourselves after the pain.

So, let this be your story too. Let these pages remind you that no matter how broken you feel, you have the strength to rebuild. That love, even when it hurts, is worth it.

Take a deep breath, turn the page, and let's begin.

1. The Dreamer Heartstrings Awakened

Suraj sat alone on his balcony, the city lights twinkling in the distance as he held his notebook close. He'd filled hundreds of pages with words that spoke to him, each verse a piece of his soul. At 22, he found his deepest connection not with people but with the lines he wove together on paper. His friends often joked about how he was an old soul, lost in a world of metaphors and rhymes, but Suraj felt it was the only way he could truly breathe.

He had always believed that one day, someone would come into his life who would understand those words, who would bring them to life. He had grown up dreaming of a love that felt like poetry, something pure and unbreakable. So he wrote, night after night, in the hopes that somehow, those words would manifest into something real.

Suraj's pen hovered over the page as he murmured the words of his latest piece:

"In the silence of my nights, I wait,

For love to knock upon my gate.

A dream, a whisper, a fleeting trace,

Of a soul whose warmth I'll embrace."

He sighed, feeling both the ache of his longing and the hope that, someday, someone would read these lines and understand the yearning they held. He imagined a soul that would walk into his life, seeing through his defenses and feeling the same inexplicable pull he felt whenever he thought about love.

He closed his notebook, glancing at the stars. Somewhere out there, he thought, there was someone who would look up at the same sky and feel the same way. Until then, he would keep writing, keep waiting, and let his words be his guide.

2. A Chance Encounter

It started innocently enough. Suraj had been scrolling through Instagram one night when a photo of a girl caught his eye. She had a bright smile and eyes that seemed to dance with life. He felt a sudden, inexplicable urge to know her story, to hear her laugh, to see that smile in person. Her name was Parvati, and with a quick swipe, he found himself on her profile, scanning through her photos and small snippets of her life.

He hesitated for a moment, his finger hovering over the "Follow" button. With a quick breath, he clicked it, not expecting anything to come from it. But when she followed him back a few hours later, his heart skipped a beat. A simple message exchange turned into hours of conversation that night, both of them talking about everything and nothing. Their words flowed easily, as though they had known each other in another life.

Soon, their conversations became a daily ritual. He found himself looking forward to those moments when his phone would light up with her messages. There was something about Parvati that felt different—she was free-spirited, vibrant, and unafraid to speak her mind. Suraj felt a spark he hadn't felt before, a pull that made him want to dive deeper into her world.

He couldn't resist expressing the wonder of it all in a new poem:

"A click, a word, a spark of flame,

And two strangers never stay the same.

A bond ignited across the air,

In digital realms, our hearts laid bare."

Suraj knew he was falling, and he didn't want to stop.

3. The First Spark

The days turned into weeks, and soon they were inseparable. Conversations became phone calls, and phone calls became plans to meet. When they finally met in person, it was as if the rest of the world had fallen away. Parvati's presence was warm, and her laughter filled the spaces in his heart that had once felt empty.

One crisp January evening, Suraj found himself standing close to her under a starlit sky, feeling his heart race as he looked into her eyes. There was a tension between them, a magnetic pull that neither could deny. Slowly, almost hesitantly, he leaned in, brushing his lips against hers. The kiss was tender, filled with both the passion and innocence of a first love. It was the kind of moment he had written about countless times, but living it was more profound than he had ever imagined.

As they pulled away, he felt a warmth spreading through him—a feeling of completeness. This was the moment he had been waiting for, the one that made all his years of writing worth it.

Later that night, he penned another poem, capturing the memory of that kiss and the promise of something beautiful:

"Lips like fire, hearts ablaze,

In your arms, I lose my gaze.

Fingers tracing paths untold,

In you, I find warmth, no longer cold."

Suraj knew then that his life had changed forever. Parvati had brought his words to life, and he felt, for the first time, that he was exactly where he was meant to be.

4. A Blossoming Romance

Days turned into months, and soon Suraj and Parvati became inseparable. They became a fixture in each other's lives, woven into the fabric of daily routines and dreams for the future. They spent countless hours exploring the city, wandering through narrow streets, and finding cozy little cafes where they could talk for hours. With each passing day, Suraj's feelings for Parvati grew stronger. He couldn't remember a time when he felt so alive, so full of purpose.

The two of them fit together so naturally, like pieces of a puzzle. Suraj found himself sharing parts of himself that he'd kept hidden from others, opening up in ways he hadn't thought possible. Parvati's spirit and spontaneity made every moment exciting. She had a way of pulling him out of his shell, helping him see the beauty in things he had once taken for granted.

One Saturday, as they wandered through a local market, Suraj looked at Parvati and felt a surge of emotion. He loved how she'd get lost in the little things—her eyes lighting up at the sight of a handmade bracelet, the way she'd laugh at the vendor's jokes, her effortless charm. Suraj felt a warmth in his chest, realizing that he was falling deeply, hopelessly in love with her.

That night, as they sat by the river, listening to the quiet sounds of the water, Suraj couldn't help but think that he had found what he'd been searching for all his life. He knew he had to express the overwhelming joy he felt in his heart. As he sat beside her, he took her hand, looked into her eyes, and recited a poem he'd written just for her:

"In every corner of this town,

Our laughter echoes, never drowns.

With every step, our love grows bold,

A story together, yet to be told."

Parvati smiled, resting her head on his shoulder as they watched the river shimmer under the moonlight. She squeezed his hand, and for a moment, Suraj felt like time had stopped. The world faded away, leaving just the two of them, wrapped in a shared silence that spoke volumes.

Yet, as the weeks went on, Suraj began to notice subtle shifts in Parvati's behaviour. Sometimes she'd withdraw, her gaze turning distant, as if she was somewhere else entirely. There were moments when she seemed distracted, almost as if something was troubling her, but every time Suraj asked, she'd brush it off with a quick smile, insisting that everything was fine.

Despite the flickers of uncertainty, Suraj pushed those thoughts aside. He didn't want anything to disrupt the happiness they'd found. He convinced himself that he was simply overthinking things, that every relationship had its ups and downs. They were in love, and that was all that mattered.

As spring gave way to summer, Suraj's birthday arrived, and Parvati surprised him with an elaborate celebration. She had planned everything down to the last detail, collaborating with his family to throw a small gathering at his favourite restaurant. When he walked in and saw the decorations, the laughter, and Parvati's bright smile, he felt overwhelmed with gratitude and love.

As the evening wore on, Parvati led him outside, away from the noise of the party. They stood under the starlit sky, her hands warm in his. She looked up at him, her eyes sparkling, and whispered, "I've never felt this way before, Suraj. I want you to know that you mean the world to me."

Suraj's heart swelled as he pulled her into his arms, feeling the weight of her words settle around him. He knew then that he would do anything to protect what they had. He would cherish every moment, every laugh, every tear. They were building something beautiful, something worth holding onto.

Later that night, after the celebration had ended and he was lying in bed, Suraj reached for his notebook. He let the pen glide across the page, pouring out the feelings he couldn't quite capture with words. His love for Parvati was growing deeper, more intense, and he knew that, despite the small shadows that sometimes appeared, he wanted this love to last.

"In the quiet hours we find our space,

Between the breaths, the love we trace.

You made my world a little bright,

With whispered love and soft sunlight."

As he set his notebook aside, Suraj closed his eyes, feeling a profound sense of peace. He fell asleep with the hope that they would continue to grow together, to share in each other's lives, and to build a future that was as bright and full of love as the dreams he carried in his heart.

5. Moments of Bliss

The days after his birthday were a whirlwind of happiness. Suraj and Parvati seemed to be closer than ever, finding joy in the simplest moments together. They would spend long afternoons exploring new places, making memories that felt like little treasures he could carry with him always. Parvati had a way of making him feel alive, of helping him see the beauty in even the smallest, most ordinary things.

One morning, she surprised him with a spontaneous road trip. They drove through rolling fields, stopping by small roadside cafes, and spending hours walking through flower fields. Parvati snapped pictures of everything—the sprawling green landscape, Suraj laughing as he twirled her around, the two of them lying in the grass and looking up at the sky. The day felt like a dream, a perfect snapshot of the love they shared.

Later that evening, as they sat in the car watching the sun set, Parvati looked at Suraj with a softness in her eyes that made his heart ache with happiness. She reached for his hand and held it tightly, her thumb brushing against his knuckles.

"I don't think I've ever been this happy," she whispered, resting her head on his shoulder.

Suraj wrapped his arms around her, feeling the warmth of her words settle deep within him. He knew he felt the same, that he had found something with her that he'd spent his whole life searching for. The world outside was bathed in the soft hues of dusk, and he felt as though they were wrapped in a cocoon of their own.

As they drove back home, Suraj let himself imagine a future with Parvati—a life filled with these moments, with laughter, with shared dreams. He could see it all so clearly, and for the first time, he allowed himself to believe that it could be real.

When he got home that night, he opened his notebook, the words flowing effortlessly as he wrote about the joy she had brought into his life:

"In the quiet hours we find our space,

Between the breaths, the love we trace.

You made my world a little bright,

With whispered love and soft sunlight."

Yet, as much as their love continued to blossom, Suraj began to notice little shifts in Parvati's behaviour. Sometimes, she would go quiet, lost in thought, her gaze distant as if she were somewhere far away. Other times, she would cancel their plans abruptly, her excuses vague and unconvincing.

He brushed these moments off, reminding himself that everyone had their off days. Love was about understanding and patience, he told himself. He knew that relationships weren't always perfect, and he was willing to accept the ups and downs that came with loving someone. But a small part of him couldn't shake the feeling that something was changing, that there were things Parvati wasn't telling him.

For her birthday in September, Suraj planned a surprise celebration, much like the one she had organized for him. He filled her room with flowers and candles, carefully arranging everything so that she would feel as special as she had made him feel. When she walked into the room, her face lit up, and for a moment, all his worries faded away.

They spent the evening laughing, dancing, and talking late into the night. Parvati's laughter filled the room, and Suraj felt a sense of contentment that he hadn't felt in weeks. As the night wore on, he reached for her phone to take a picture of them together, but she quickly pulled it away, a flicker of panic crossing her face. She handed it back to him a moment later, but the expression lingered, unsettling him.

He tried to push the thought away, but it gnawed at him, a tiny seed of doubt that had taken root. He wanted to believe that everything was fine, that they were still as close as they had always been, but something about that moment stayed with him, lingering in the back of his mind.

A few days later, one of Suraj's friends pulled him aside, a concerned look on his face. He had overheard Parvati talking to her ex-boyfriend, he said, the conversation seeming a little too friendly. Suraj's heart clenched as he listened, feeling a wave of fear and confusion crash over him. When he confronted Parvati about it, she brushed it off at first, but eventually, she admitted to talking to her ex, insisting that it was just a casual conversation.

Suraj tried to let it go, reminding himself that trust was the foundation of any relationship. But as the days passed, more cracks began to appear. Parvati would disappear for hours, and when he asked where she had been, her answers were vague, her tone defensive. Their conversations, once filled with laughter and ease, became strained, as though there was a barrier between them that neither could break.

He poured his frustrations into his poetry, hoping that the words would help him make sense of the chaos in his heart:

"In love's bright glow, a shadow fell,

A doubt that neither could dispel.

In trust, we place our fragile heart,

But cracks can tear the trust apart."

Despite the growing tension, Suraj clung to the hope that they could work things out. He believed in the love they had built, in the memories they had created, and he was willing to fight to keep it. But deep down, he knew that something had changed, and he couldn't shake the feeling that the love he had dreamed of was slipping away.

6. Cracks in the Foundation

Suraj spent the next few weeks trying to ignore the doubts gnawing at his mind. He wanted to believe that he and Parvati could work through whatever was creating this rift between them. He told himself it was just a phase, that things would go back to the way they were. But the nagging feeling of unease grew harder to ignore with each passing day.

One sunny afternoon, he invited her for a day out. He wanted to recreate one of their first dates, hoping it would remind them both of the love they had built together. They wandered through the city, visited their favourite spots, and eventually found themselves at a quiet park where they sat down to talk. Suraj felt the familiar comfort of being with her, but the shadow in his heart remained.

As they sat in the warm sunlight, he decided to confront the doubts that had been tormenting him. He turned to her and asked, "Parvati, are we okay? It feels like something's different lately."

She hesitated, her eyes darting away before she forced a smile. "Of course we are, Suraj. I'm just… I don't know, things have been a little stressful, I guess. But that has nothing to do with us."

He wanted to believe her, but there was something in her voice that didn't sit right. He pushed the thoughts aside, unwilling to press further. Instead, he took her hand and squeezed it, hoping that his silent support would be enough.

The following week, Suraj decided to plan another surprise for her—this time, a small dinner at a cozy restaurant they'd both wanted to try. He wanted to show her that he was committed to making their relationship work, that he would be there for her no matter what.

As they sat down to dinner, he noticed that Parvati seemed distracted, glancing at her phone more than usual. She apologized, saying it was work-related messages, but he couldn't help but feel a pang of frustration. He wanted to have her full attention, just for one night.

Trying to shake off the feeling, he reminded himself of the love they had shared. He looked at her across the table, the candlelight casting soft shadows on her face, and reached for her hand. "Let's put our phones away tonight," he suggested, smiling. "Let's just be here, together."

She hesitated, glancing at her phone one last time before setting it down. They enjoyed a lovely dinner, but Suraj couldn't shake the feeling that something was off. Parvati seemed present, but there was a distance in her eyes that hadn't been there before.

One evening in late September, Suraj planned a small gathering for her birthday. He filled the room with balloons, candles, and her favourite flowers, hoping to recreate the magic of the celebration she had organized for him. She arrived, and her face lit up with delight. They laughed, danced, and shared quiet moments, wrapped in the warmth of each other's presence.

As the night wound down, Parvati reached for her phone to capture a picture of the two of them. She handed it to Suraj to take a photo, but just as he was about to press the button, a message notification appeared. He caught a glimpse of the name, his heart dropping as he recognized it—it was her ex-boyfriend.

He handed the phone back, trying to mask his discomfort, but the moment stayed with him, unsettling him. That small instance opened a flood of insecurities, questions he hadn't allowed himself to ask.

The next day, he found the courage to bring it up. "Parvati," he started, keeping his voice calm, "I saw that your ex texted you last night. Is everything okay?"

She frowned, clearly uncomfortable. "Oh, that… it was nothing, really. Just a casual hello. I didn't think it was a big deal."

But to Suraj, it was a big deal. He felt a sting of betrayal, an unspoken understanding that she had kept something from him. Yet, he tried to convince himself that it wasn't worth making a fuss over. Everyone had a past, he reminded himself. He didn't want to be the insecure boyfriend who couldn't handle a simple text message.

Days later, however, a mutual friend mentioned seeing Parvati talking to her ex in person. Suraj's heart pounded with anxiety as he heard this, and that night, he confronted her again. This time, she reacted defensively, anger flashing in her eyes.

"Why are you being so controlling, Suraj? He's just a friend now. You're the one I'm with!" Her words stung, and he found himself speechless, unsure of how to respond. He didn't want to be controlling, but he also couldn't ignore the ache in his heart, the feeling that something wasn't right.

Despite her reassurances, Suraj couldn't help but feel the cracks widening. Parvati became increasingly distant, her mood shifts unpredictable. They argued more often, small misunderstandings escalating into tense confrontations. She would accuse him of being possessive, of not trusting her, and he would find himself apologizing, desperate to hold onto what they had.

He tried to brush aside his doubts, convincing himself that love was about compromise. But in quiet moments, when he was alone, the truth gnawed at him, relentless and undeniable. His once-perfect love story was becoming fractured, and he felt powerless to stop it.

He poured his feelings into his notebook, letting his pain flow through the ink as he wrote:

"In love's bright glow, a shadow fell,

A doubt that neither could dispel.

In trust, we place our fragile heart,

But cracks can tear the trust apart."

As he closed his notebook, Suraj knew that he had to face the reality he'd been avoiding. Their relationship was no longer the safe haven it had once been. He wanted to save what they had, but he feared it was slipping further from his grasp with each passing day.

7. The Breakup

The weeks that followed felt like a slow descent into an inevitable heartbreak. Suraj clung to the memories they had made, hoping that the love he and Parvati shared would be enough to mend the growing rift between them. But despite his efforts, the distance between them only widened, the warmth they once shared fading into an unsettling coldness.

It was a chilly October evening when it all came crashing down. Suraj had invited Parvati to his favourite spot by the river—a place where they had often gone to escape the noise of the city. The two of them sat in silence, the once-comforting quiet now tinged with tension. Suraj searched her face, hoping for a glimmer of the warmth he remembered, but she looked away, her expression guarded.

Finally, he gathered the courage to speak. "Parvati, I can't shake this feeling that something's changed. I know we've been going through a rough patch, but I'm willing to do whatever it takes to make things right. I just need you to be honest with me."

She took a deep breath, and he saw a flicker of sadness cross her face. "Suraj… I don't know if I feel the same way anymore. I'm sorry. I didn't want to hurt you, but I can't pretend that everything's fine."

His heart plummeted as he processed her words. He had feared this moment, but hearing it from her shattered him in a way he hadn't anticipated. He struggled to find the right words, his mind reeling with questions, with a desperate need to understand what had gone wrong.

"But… why?" he managed, his voice barely a whisper. "I thought we were building something real. I thought we were happy."

Parvati looked away, her expression a mixture of guilt and frustration. "I don't know, Suraj. Things just… changed. Maybe it's my fault, or maybe we were just different from the start. I need space to figure things out."

He reached for her hand, hoping that his touch would remind her of the love they had shared, but she pulled away, creating a chasm between them that felt impossible to bridge. His mind raced, memories flashing before him—the laughter, the moments of pure joy, the promises they had made.

"Please," he pleaded, "let's work on this together. We can figure it out. I'll do whatever it takes."

Parvati's gaze softened, but her resolve remained unshaken. "I'm sorry, Suraj. I think this is for the best. Maybe it's time we both moved on."

Her words were like a knife to his heart, slicing through the hope he had clung to so tightly. He tried to reason with her, to remind her of the love they had built, but she remained distant, her expression unyielding. It was as if she had already made up her mind, leaving him no choice but to accept the painful truth.

When she walked away that evening, Suraj felt a wave of despair wash over him, the weight of her absence settling heavily on his shoulders. He watched her retreating figure until she disappeared from view, leaving him alone with the remnants of their shattered love.

In the days that followed, Suraj struggled to make sense of the breakup. He replayed their final conversation over and over in his mind, searching for clues, for any indication that he could have prevented it. He had always believed that love could conquer any obstacle, that with enough effort and patience, they could have overcome the challenges that had torn them apart.

But the reality was stark and unforgiving. Parvati had chosen to walk away, leaving him with a hollow ache that he didn't know how to fill. He reached out to her a few times, hoping that she would reconsider, that she would remember the love they had shared and give their relationship another chance. But each time, she grew colder, her responses curt and dismissive.

One evening, Suraj discovered through a mutual friend that Parvati had started spending time with her ex-boyfriends, even dating one of her seniors. The news hit him like a punch to the gut, a betrayal that he hadn't anticipated. He had always trusted her, believing that their love was strong enough to withstand any temptation, but her actions revealed a side of her he hadn't seen before.

Unable to contain his frustration, he confronted her, hoping for an explanation that would ease his pain. But Parvati only looked at him with disdain, dismissing his hurt as if it were inconsequential. Her words cut deeper than any wound, her indifference a painful reminder of how far they had drifted apart.

"You need to move on, Suraj," she said, her voice cold and unfeeling. "I don't owe you anything. It's over, and you need to accept that."

In that moment, Suraj realised that the woman he had loved so deeply was gone, replaced by someone he no longer recognized. The love they had shared was now a distant memory, and he was left with nothing but the fragments of his shattered heart.

Consumed by grief, Suraj turned to the one solace he had always found comfort in—his poetry. He poured his pain into his words, each verse a reflection of the love he had lost, the betrayal he had endured. Writing became his lifeline, a way to process the overwhelming emotions that threatened to drown him.

He filled his notebook with poems of heartache, each line a testament to the love he had once believed in so fervently:

"The love we built, so strong, so true,

Now fades away, like morning dew.

A whisper, a sigh, a final plea,

But love once lost, can never be."

As he wrote, he found a strange sense of catharsis in the act of expressing his pain. The words became his refuge, a way to release the anguish that had taken root in his heart. He knew that he could never erase the love he had shared with Parvati, but he hoped that in time, he would find a way to heal, to rebuild the pieces of himself that had been shattered.

The days turned into weeks, and while the pain remained, Suraj began to find solace in the small moments of peace that writing brought him. He realised that, though his heart was broken, he still had the strength to carry on. He had lost a part of himself, but he was determined to rebuild, to find meaning in the scars that Parvati had left behind.

8. Writing the Pain

In the aftermath of the breakup, Suraj was plunged into a period of profound grief and isolation. The dreams of a future with Parvati lay shattered, leaving him to grapple with a void that seemed impossible to fill. Memories of their time together clung to him, surfacing in the smallest, most unexpected moments: the lyrics of a favorite song, the sight of her favorite book on his shelf, or the quiet evenings where his instinct was still to reach for his phone to text her. Each memory was a dagger, a reminder of what he had lost.

Yet, amidst this storm of heartbreak, someone entered Suraj's life who would become his beacon of light—a golden retriever named Barfi. Suraj adopted Barfi on an impulse, hoping for some distraction from the overwhelming pain. What he received was far more profound. Barfi's boundless energy and unconditional love became a salve for Suraj's wounded heart. Whether it was the joyful wag of his tail or the way he would rest his head on Suraj's lap when he sensed his sadness, Barfi became an anchor in the chaos.

One cold evening, Suraj sat at his desk, staring at a blank notebook page. Barfi lay curled up at his feet, his soft golden fur a comfort against the harsh reality of solitude. A deep urge stirred within Suraj—an urge to write, to release the storm of emotions swirling inside him. He picked up his pen, and as the ink flowed across the page, so did the tears he had held back for too long. The words came tumbling out, raw and unfiltered, capturing the depth of his heartbreak and confusion.

Ink of Pain

"In every line, I bleed, I cry,

The words are all that's left of why.

For love once sweet, now turned to dust,

In words, I seek the strength to trust."

Writing became Suraj's refuge. His notebook turned into a mirror of his soul, reflecting every stage of his mourning. He poured out the memories, the laughter, and the tenderness, but also the moments of doubt, the misunderstandings, and the pain of her absence. Each poem was a small act of survival, a step forward on a path he wasn't sure he could walk.

Barfi became his silent companion through this journey. On nights when the weight of grief felt unbearable, Barfi would nuzzle his hand, pulling him back from the brink. On mornings when getting out of bed felt impossible, Barfi's eager barks and playful antics gave Suraj a reason to keep moving. In Barfi, Suraj found a love so pure and unconditional that it began to mend the broken pieces of his heart.

Paws of Healing

"With golden fur and gentle eyes,

You mend the heart that aches and cries.

Your wagging tail, a balm so true,

In every step, you pull me through."

As the weeks turned into months, Suraj began to notice a shift within himself. Through his writing and Barfi's unwavering presence, he was beginning to find clarity. The act of putting his emotions into words allowed him to process the relationship's end. He started to reflect on the ways he had idealized Parvati, how he had ignored the red flags, and how his own insecurities had contributed to their downfall.

Suraj filled page after page with poems that chronicled his journey. Some verses stung with the sharpness of fresh wounds, while others hinted at a growing sense of peace. Through this process, he discovered a surprising strength within himself. He began to understand that his pain, while immense, was also a testament to his capacity to love deeply.

One evening, as he reread the poems he had written since the breakup, Suraj felt a strange sense of accomplishment. His notebook was no longer just a collection of grief-stricken words; it was a testament to his resilience. It captured his journey from heartbreak to healing, from despair to hope.

Acceptance "I loved you once, and that was true,

But now I let the past slip through.

The weight I carried, the tears I shed,

I lay them down; our story's read."

Suraj closed the notebook and placed it on his desk, a small smile playing on his lips. He looked down at Barfi, who was now sprawled out on the floor, snoring softly. He knelt beside him, running his fingers through his fur. "Thank you, buddy," he whispered. "For everything."

The road ahead was still uncertain, and Suraj knew he wasn't entirely healed. But he also knew he wasn't walking it alone. With his pen in one hand and Barfi by his side, he was ready to keep moving forward, one step and one poem at a time.

9. An Unexpected Reunion

Months passed, and though the raw edges of Suraj's heartbreak had begun to soften, loneliness still lingered. His days were a delicate balance of healing and reliving memories, but his golden retriever, Barfi, became the companion he never knew he needed. Barfi's wagging tail and boundless energy brought light into the darkest corners of Suraj's days. Every morning, Barfi would nuzzle him awake, his soulful eyes filled with unconditional love, reminding Suraj that he wasn't alone.

In his quiet moments, Suraj often sat with Barfi by his side, writing poetry while stroking his soft fur. The dog seemed to sense his pain and would place a gentle paw on his lap whenever he felt overwhelmed. Barfi had become his anchor, a constant reminder that love could be simple and pure.

"Paws of Healing"

"In your eyes, I find the light,

A love so pure, it feels just right.

Your wagging tail, your gentle gaze,

Have healed my heart in countless ways."

One evening, as Suraj scrolled through Instagram, a notification appeared. It was a message from Disha, an old school friend of Parvati's. She had come across one of his poems and reached out with words of encouragement. Though hesitant at first, Suraj responded, and soon their casual chat turned into heartfelt conversations.

Their exchanges became a regular part of his evenings. While Barfi lay curled at his feet, Suraj found himself opening up to Disha about his struggles and the lingering pain from his breakup. Her warmth and understanding felt genuine, and he appreciated the comfort she offered.

After weeks of talking, Disha invited him for coffee. Suraj was initially unsure but decided to step out of his comfort zone. Barfi seemed to sense his nervousness that morning and nudged him playfully, as if to say, "You've got this."

At the café, Disha greeted him with a radiant smile. Her presence was warm, her laughter infectious, and for the first time in months, Suraj felt at ease with someone new. They talked about everything—their childhood memories, dreams, and even the unexpected twists life had thrown their way.

As their bond deepened, Disha encouraged Suraj to channel his emotions into poetry about the future, rather than the past. Her words planted a seed of hope in his heart, but Suraj remained cautious. While he valued their connection, his heart still bore the weight of Parvati's memories.

Barfi became a silent witness to Suraj's journey. Whenever Disha visited, Barfi would wag his tail enthusiastically, almost as if he approved of her presence. Disha, in turn, showered Barfi with affection, often bringing him treats or playing fetch with him in the park.

One evening, as Suraj and Disha walked by the river, she admitted her growing feelings for him. While touched by her honesty, Suraj wasn't ready to move forward romantically. "I care about you deeply, Disha," he said, "but my heart is still healing. I hope you can understand."

Disha smiled softly. "I do, Suraj. I just wanted to be honest. Whether as a friend or something more, I'm here for you."

Their friendship continued to grow, strengthened by mutual respect and understanding. Barfi's playful antics often lightened their moments together, his presence a constant reminder of love's simple joys.

One evening, inspired by his journey and Barfi's unwavering love, Suraj penned a poem that captured his newfound sense of peace:

"Second Chances"

"Through shadows deep, I found my way,

With paws beside me every day.

A bond unspoken, pure and true,

In Barfi's love, I start anew."

As Suraj closed his notebook, Barfi placed his head on his lap, looking up at him with trusting eyes. Suraj smiled, feeling a quiet sense of gratitude. The road ahead might still hold challenges, but with Barfi by his side and friends like Disha in his corner, he felt ready to embrace the possibilities of tomorrow.

10. Embracing Self-Love

As the months passed, Suraj's life began to take on a new rhythm. He still saw Disha often, finding comfort in her companionship, but he was also starting to find solace in himself. The days no longer felt heavy with longing; instead, they felt open, filled with possibilities he hadn't seen before.

Suraj had begun to focus on his own growth. He attended poetry workshops, reconnecting with his love for words. He joined a local reading group and started meditating each morning, letting the stillness bring him a sense of inner peace. For the first time in his life, he wasn't seeking validation from someone else—he was learning to appreciate the person he was becoming.

One evening, as he and Disha were sitting in a small bookstore, surrounded by shelves of books that seemed to echo the stories of countless lives, she asked him a question that made him pause.

"Suraj, do you think you'll ever be able to fully let go of Parvati?"

He looked at her, considering the question carefully. "I don't know if I'll ever completely forget her. She was a part of my life, and that won't change. But I've realised that holding onto the pain won't bring her back, and it won't heal me either. I need to let go, not for her, but for myself."

Disha nodded, her gaze steady. "I'm proud of you, you know. It takes strength to let go, especially when you've loved so deeply."

Suraj smiled, feeling a warmth in his chest. He knew she meant every word, and it gave him the courage to continue on this journey of self-discovery.

As Suraj spent more time alone, he began to explore parts of himself that he had neglected during his relationship with Parvati. He found joy in the little things—morning walks in the park, savouring a cup of coffee at a quiet café, watching the sun set over the city skyline. These moments became small reminders that happiness didn't have to come from another person; it could be found within himself, in the beauty of the world around him.

One day, he attended a poetry workshop focused on self-love and healing. The instructor asked the group to write a letter to themselves, expressing forgiveness and compassion. Suraj hesitated, feeling the familiar weight of doubt rise within him. But as he put pen to paper, he found the words flowing, an unexpected release that brought a sense of clarity he hadn't anticipated.

Letter to Himself:

"Dear Suraj,

You've walked a path filled with pain, but you've also found strength in that journey. You loved with all your heart, and even though it ended, that doesn't mean you failed. It just means that love is a lesson, one that sometimes teaches us to let go.

You are enough, just as you are. You don't need to prove yourself to anyone. Be gentle with yourself, forgive yourself for the mistakes you made, and trust that you deserve happiness.

With love,

Yourself"

After reading the letter, he felt a deep sense of relief. He realised he had been holding onto guilt and self-doubt, but now he was ready to forgive himself. He folded the letter and placed it in his notebook, a reminder of the progress he had made and the journey he was still on.

A few weeks later, Suraj and Disha went out for dinner. They shared their favourite memories from childhood, laughed over embarrassing stories, and talked about their dreams for the future. But as the evening drew on, their conversation took a more serious turn.

"Suraj," Disha began, her eyes reflecting a mixture of vulnerability and hope, "I need to tell you something. I've really come to care for you, and I think... I think I've fallen for you. But I don't want to be someone you turn to just because you're trying to move on from someone else. I need to know that if we start something, it's because you're ready for it."

Suraj felt a lump in his throat, her words stirring emotions he hadn't fully addressed. He looked into her eyes, seeing the sincerity there, and he knew she deserved an honest answer.

"Disha, you've become such an important part of my life, and I care about you too. But I think there's a part of me that still hasn't fully healed. I don't want to enter into a relationship unless I'm certain I can give it my all. You mean too much to me to be anything less than honest."

Disha reached out, placing a reassuring hand on his. "Thank you for telling me the truth. I'm here for you, Suraj, no matter what. Take all the time you need."

Suraj nodded, grateful for her understanding. That night, as he walked home alone, he reflected on their conversation. He knew that healing wasn't a linear process, but he felt a sense of peace knowing that he could take things one step at a time. He wasn't alone on this journey, and he had people who cared for him—people who believed in him even when he struggled to believe in himself.

In the days that followed, Suraj continued to focus on his self-growth. He read books on mindfulness, practiced yoga, and immersed himself in the art of poetry. He found a new community of friends who shared his passion for writing, and through them, he began to see his life from a fresh perspective. One evening, he sat down to write a poem, feeling the words rise within him like a quiet strength he hadn't known he possessed.

"To Myself"

"I am enough, in every way,
The love I seek, I'll find today.
Not in the arms of someone new,

But in my heart, where love is true."

As he read the poem aloud, he felt a surge of empowerment. He had spent so long seeking love from others, but now he understood that true love started from within. It was a lesson that had taken him months to learn, but he was grateful for every step of the journey.

Suraj knew there would be days when the memories of Parvati would return, days when he would still feel the ache of what could have been. But he was no longer afraid of that pain. He could welcome it as part of his story, knowing that it had shaped him into the person he was becoming.

He looked at his reflection in the mirror, a soft smile spreading across his face. He was ready to embrace the next chapter of his life, a chapter he would write on his own terms. For the first time in a long time, he felt a sense of wholeness, a sense of peace that came from within. He was ready to let go of the past and step into the future, knowing that he had the strength to carry himself forward.

11. Learning from Heartbreak

As the sun dipped below the horizon, casting a golden glow through his window, Suraj found himself sitting at his desk, surrounded by scattered notes and crumpled pages. The quiet of the evening settled around him, a stark contrast to the chaos of emotions he felt inside. It was time to confront the whirlwind of thoughts that had consumed him for so long.

Suraj opened his notebook, the one he had filled with poems and reflections during his relationship with Parvati. He flipped through the pages, skimming over lines that once brought him joy but now echoed with pain. He paused at a poem he had written right after their breakup. The words felt heavy, filled with longing and despair, yet they also marked a turning point in his journey.

Taking a deep breath, he began to write again. This time, he focused not on the heartbreak, but on the lessons he had learned. His pen glided across the paper as he poured out his thoughts:

"The Lesson of Love"

"In loss, I found my way again,

Through heartbreak's storm, I felt the rain.

Each drop a teacher, each tear a guide,

To the love I carry now inside."

"With every scar, a story told,

Of dreams once bright, now a bit old.

Yet from the ashes, I rise anew,

For love, dear love, begins with you."

"I've learned that trust can bend and break,

But from the pain, I choose to wake.

To honor what was, yet not be confined,

To love myself, for I am kind."

"So here's my heart, I offer it free,

Not seeking others to define me.

For in my soul, I find my song,

A melody of self-love, where I belong."

Suraj read the poem aloud, feeling the power of his words resonate within him. It was cathartic, a release of emotions that had been bottled up for too long. Each line echoed with newfound strength, a declaration of his intent to embrace self-love and the lessons that came from his heartache.

In the following weeks, Suraj continued to focus on his healing journey. He explored new hobbies, like painting and hiking, allowing himself to experience life beyond poetry. He began to understand that healing wasn't just about writing; it was about living fully and immersing himself in new experiences.

One sunny afternoon, he decided to take a hike at a nearby nature reserve. The vibrant colors of the trees and the crisp air invigorated him as he walked along the winding paths. It felt like a rebirth, a chance to breathe and reconnect with himself.

He took a moment to sit on a large rock overlooking a serene lake, the water shimmering in the sunlight.

As he sat there, he reflected on his journey. The weight of his past no longer felt like a burden; instead, it was a chapter in his story, shaping him into who he was becoming. Suraj realised that it was okay to carry the memories of Parvati with him, as long as they didn't define him.

Back at home, he found himself seeking solace in his poetry community. Suraj joined a local open mic night, where he had the opportunity to share his work with others. The first time he stood in front of an audience, his heart raced with nerves. But as he recited his poems, he felt an exhilarating sense of liberation wash over him.

The supportive cheers and applause from the crowd filled him with confidence. For the first time in a long while, he felt seen and appreciated for who he was—not just as Parvati's boyfriend, but as Suraj, a poet and an individual with a story to tell.

After his reading, he spoke with a few fellow writers who shared their experiences of love and loss. They offered words of encouragement and camaraderie, reinforcing his belief that he wasn't alone in this journey.

One evening, Disha invited him over for a casual dinner. As they sat on her balcony, sipping tea and watching the stars emerge in the night sky, Suraj felt a sense of ease. Disha was easy to talk to, and their conversations flowed effortlessly, without the weight of expectations or past heartbreak.

"Suraj," she said, her voice gentle, "I can see how much you've grown over these past months. It's inspiring to watch you embrace this journey."

Suraj smiled, feeling grateful for her presence. "I think I'm finally understanding what it means to love myself. It's a process, but I'm getting there."

Disha's eyes sparkled with understanding. "You deserve that love, Suraj. I believe in you."

Suraj felt a warmth spread through him. While he wasn't ready for a romantic relationship, he valued Disha's friendship deeply. It was comforting to have someone who encouraged him to be vulnerable and honest.

As the chapter progressed, Suraj dedicated himself to writing a new collection of poems that celebrated self-love and healing. He envisioned it as a journey from heartbreak to empowerment, a testament to the resilience of the human spirit. Each poem reflected his growth, allowing him to process his feelings while inspiring others who might be navigating their own heartaches.

Finally, he penned a poem he felt encapsulated his journey, a reflection of the strength he had discovered within himself.

"A Heart Reclaimed"

"With every tear that stained my face,

I learned to find my sacred space.

The wounds I bore, the scars I claim,

Are part of me, not a source of shame."

"I rise from ashes, fierce and free,

A heart reclaimed, it belongs to me.
For love is vast, it shifts and flows,
And in its current, my spirit grows."
Suraj closed his notebook, feeling a sense of accomplishment. He had come so far from the boy who once believed that love could only be found in someone else. Now, he understood that love was multifaceted and began within his own heart.

As he prepared for bed that night, Suraj felt a profound sense of peace settle over him. The journey ahead remained uncertain, but he was ready to embrace it. He was no longer defined by his past; he was ready to write his future, one poem at a time.

12. A Poem of Closure

The air was thick with anticipation as Suraj prepared to write a poem that he had both longed for and dreaded. It had been nearly a year since Parvati had walked out of his life, leaving behind a trail of confusion and heartache. Now, as he sat at his desk with a fresh notebook in front of him, he knew it was time to bring closure to that chapter.

Suraj glanced out the window, watching the gentle sway of the trees outside. The world seemed alive with possibility, a stark contrast to the heaviness that had once weighed him down. He took a deep breath, closed his eyes, and reflected on the journey that had led him to this moment.

He thought about the first spark of love he had felt when he met Parvati, the joy of their blossoming romance, and ultimately, the pain of their breakup. Each memory was like a brushstroke on a canvas, contributing to the intricate painting of his experience. But now, it was time to put down the paintbrush and step back, appreciating the entire masterpiece without dwelling on the colors that had faded.

Suraj picked up his pen and began to write, pouring his heart into the page:

"Farewell to You"

"In every breath, I loved you true,
But now it's time to bid adieu.

Our chapter's done, the story told,

In letting go, I'm finally whole."

"The laughter shared, the dreams we spun,

In the tapestry of us, we had our fun.

But threads can fray, and colors can bleed,

And from the ashes, I plant a new seed."

"With every tear that carved my soul,

I learned to rise, I learned to be whole.

The love we built was a beautiful start,

But now I reclaim my wandering heart."

"I thank you for the lessons learned,

For the passion felt, for the love I yearned.

But now I see, with clarity bright,

That loving myself is my true light."

"So farewell to you, my bittersweet past,

I cherish the moments, though they couldn't last.

In the journey of life, I'll carry you near,

But it's time to move on, my path is now clear."

Suraj read the poem aloud, his voice steady but tinged with emotion. Each line resonated with a sense of finality, a farewell to the love that had once consumed him. He felt lighter with every word, as if he were shedding a weight he had carried for too long.

That evening, he decided to go for a walk, hoping to find a place where he could release the poem into the universe. He wandered to the local park, where the sunset painted the sky in hues of orange and pink, casting a warm glow over the landscape.

Finding a quiet spot near the lake, he sat on a bench, the water rippling gently in front of him. Suraj took a moment to reflect on everything he had experienced—the joy, the heartbreak, and the growth. He closed his eyes and let the cool breeze wash over him, embracing the serenity of the moment.

With the notebook in hand, he stood and faced the lake, allowing the calmness of the water to absorb his words. "This is for you, Parvati," he whispered. "Thank you for the lessons, but it's time to let go."

He read the poem aloud, feeling the vibrations of his voice mingling with the rustle of leaves and the chirping of evening crickets. Each line echoed across the water, as if carrying his message into the world.

When he finished, Suraj took a deep breath, closing the notebook with a satisfying thud. It felt as if he had released a balloon into the sky, watching it drift away until it disappeared into the horizon. The ache in his heart had transformed into a soft, bittersweet remembrance—one that he could cherish without letting it define him.

As he made his way back home, he felt a renewed sense of purpose. Writing the poem had marked the end of a significant chapter, but it also signaled the beginning of a new one. Suraj was ready to embrace the future, armed with the wisdom he had gained from his past.

That night, as he lay in bed, Suraj couldn't help but smile. He felt a shift within him, a dawning realization that he was not just a poet defined by his past heartaches but a storyteller who could weave experiences into something beautiful and transformative.

In his heart, he knew there would be more love, more stories to tell, and more poems to write. But for now, he relished the freedom that came from closure. Suraj drifted off to sleep, dreaming of a world filled with endless possibilities, where love—whether for oneself or for others—could flourish without fear.

13. Moving Forward

The days following the writing of his farewell poem felt like a gentle rebirth for Suraj. Each morning greeted him with renewed energy, and he awoke with a sense of purpose. It was as if a fog had lifted, revealing a vibrant landscape of possibilities ahead.

Suraj immersed himself in new experiences, eager to embrace life without the shadows of his past. He began volunteering at a local community center, where he taught poetry to children. Their laughter and unfiltered creativity reminded him of the joy that writing could bring. Each session felt like a celebration of words, and he found himself inspired by their innocence and passion.

One sunny Saturday, as he gathered with the children under a sprawling banyan tree, Suraj prompted them to write about their dreams. "What do you want to be when you grow up?" he asked, watching their faces light up with excitement.

"I want to be an astronaut!" shouted a boy with messy hair, his eyes sparkling with wonder.

"I want to be a chef and make the biggest pizza ever!" declared a girl, her hands mimicking the act of tossing dough.

As the children scribbled their dreams, Suraj reflected on his own aspirations. He had always wanted to publish a collection of his poetry. With each passing day, that dream felt more achievable.

One evening, after a fulfilling day at the community center, Suraj returned home and opened his notebook. Inspired by the children's enthusiasm, he began drafting poems for his upcoming collection. This new work focused not only on love but also on hope, dreams, and the beauty of self-discovery. Each line poured out of him, capturing the essence of life's journey and the lessons he had learned along the way.

As the weeks passed, Suraj grew more connected to his craft. He attended local poetry readings, sharing his new pieces and receiving encouragement from fellow writers. With every word he shared, he felt more like himself—less defined by heartbreak and more as an artist crafting his narrative.

One evening, after a particularly spirited open mic session, Suraj was approached by Maya, a fellow poet he had seen perform multiple times. She was vibrant and passionate about her art, with an infectious energy that drew him in.

"Your poems are beautiful," she said, her eyes shining. "You have a way of capturing emotions that resonates deeply. I'd love to collaborate on a project sometime."

Suraj felt a thrill at her suggestion. "I'd love that! I think we could create something really special together."

Their collaboration blossomed over the next few months. They met regularly at cafes, surrounded by the aroma of coffee and the buzz of conversation. They shared ideas, critiqued each other's work, and inspired one another to delve deeper into their art. Suraj found himself invigorated by Maya's perspective; she encouraged him to explore themes of vulnerability and resilience in new ways.

As they spent more time together, Suraj began to notice a budding friendship turning into something more. Maya's laughter was like music, and her insights about life sparked a flame within him that he hadn't felt in a long time. Yet, he hesitated to pursue those feelings, still wary of getting hurt again.

One evening, after a productive writing session, they decided to take a walk through the city streets, where twinkling lights adorned the sidewalks. The atmosphere was charged with a sense of possibility. Suraj felt alive as they strolled side by side, discussing their dreams and aspirations.

"Maya," Suraj began, pausing to gaze at her, "I've learned so much about love and loss in the past year. It's been a journey, but I think I'm finally ready to open my heart again."

Maya looked at him, her expression softening. "Suraj, that's beautiful. It takes a lot of courage to let go of the past and embrace what's in front of you."

Encouraged by her words, Suraj took a leap of faith. "I really enjoy spending time with you, and I'd like to see where this could go—if you're open to it."

Maya smiled, a spark of understanding passing between them. "I feel the same way. I think we could create something amazing, both in our art and together."

Their connection deepened over the following weeks, blossoming into a romance that felt refreshing and genuine.

Suraj was amazed at how easily they meshed, as if they had known each other for much longer than just a few months. They shared late-night conversations, exploring not only their dreams as poets but also their hopes for the future.

Despite the joy he felt, Suraj sometimes battled moments of insecurity. Would he be able to love again without the shadows of his past creeping in? He had to remind himself that healing was an ongoing process.

One night, while working late at his desk, he paused to write down his thoughts in a new poem:

"Opening Up"

"With every heartbeat, I learn to trust,

To embrace the unknown, it's a must.

For love, though fragile, can be a guide,

A light that leads, a friend beside."

"I step into the warmth of today,

Leaving behind the fears that sway.

For in the dance of hearts, we find,

That love, dear love, can be so kind."

Suraj felt a sense of relief as he penned those lines, allowing his vulnerability to seep onto the page. It was a reminder that he was not alone in this journey and that he had the power to create his own narrative.

As he continued to move forward, Suraj also made it a point to check in with himself regularly. He engaged in self-reflection, attending workshops and reading books on emotional intelligence. He recognized the importance of understanding his emotions, not only to grow as a poet but also to cultivate healthy relationships moving forward.

The months flew by, and Suraj's poetry collection began to take shape. It was a reflection of his journey from heartbreak to healing, and he felt proud of the progress he had made. With Maya by his side, encouraging and challenging him, he felt ready to share his work with the world.

One evening, as they sat on the balcony, sipping tea and watching the stars, Suraj turned to Maya. "I think I'm ready to publish my collection. I want to share my story, the lessons I've learned, and the beauty of moving on."

Maya's eyes lit up with excitement. "That's incredible, Suraj! You have a gift, and the world deserves to hear your voice. I'll be right here to support you every step of the way."

Suraj smiled, his heart swelling with gratitude. With every passing day, he felt more grounded in who he was and what he wanted. The scars of his past would always be a part of him, but they no longer defined him. Instead, they were the foundation upon which he built his future—one filled with love, creativity, and endless possibilities.

14. The Launch

As Suraj prepared for the launch of his poetry collection, he felt a whirlwind of emotions—excitement, anxiety, and an overwhelming sense of hope. After months of hard work, his dream of sharing his journey through words was finally becoming a reality. The book, titled "From Heartbreak to Healing: A Poet's Journey," encapsulated everything he had experienced over the past year and the lessons he had learned along the way.

With Maya's support, he organized a launch event at a local art gallery, a space that resonated with creativity and warmth. Suraj envisioned an evening filled with laughter, tears, and connection—an opportunity for him to share not only his poetry but also the story behind it.

In the days leading up to the event, he poured over the details—selecting poems to read, designing promotional materials, and inviting friends and family. Maya helped him every step of the way, her enthusiasm infectious. They spent evenings working together, surrounded by stacks of notebooks and cups of steaming tea, discussing every aspect of the launch.

"Suraj, remember to breathe. You're sharing your story, and that's a beautiful thing," Maya reminded him as they sat in a cozy café, their fingers wrapped around warm mugs.

"I know, but what if no one connects with my poems? What if they don't resonate?" he replied, his brow furrowed with concern.

"Then you've still accomplished something incredible. You've poured your heart into this, and that alone is worth celebrating. Just focus on sharing your truth," she encouraged, giving his hand a reassuring squeeze.

As the event day approached, the gallery buzzed with anticipation. Suraj arrived early to set up, his heart racing with a mixture of excitement and nerves. The walls were adorned with beautiful artwork, and fairy lights hung above, casting a warm glow that made the space feel magical. Friends and family began to trickle in, filling the room with laughter and conversation.

When the time for his reading arrived, Suraj took a deep breath, standing behind the microphone. He looked out at the audience—familiar faces mixed with new ones, all gathered to support him.

"Thank you all for being here today," Suraj began, his voice steadying as he spoke. "This collection is not just a reflection of my experiences but a testament to the power of love, loss, and healing. It's about finding the beauty in heartbreak and learning to embrace life anew."

He began to read some of his poems, feeling the words resonate deeply within him as he shared pieces from his journey. Each line carried the weight of his past, but also the lightness of newfound hope. Suraj could see the audience nodding, their expressions shifting from contemplation to warmth as they connected with his words.

After he finished reading, the room erupted into applause, and Suraj felt a wave of gratitude wash over him. He had laid bare his heart, and it had been met with acceptance and understanding.

Following the reading, Suraj mingled with guests, chatting and sharing stories. Maya stood nearby, her smile radiant as she engaged with others. She had been instrumental in helping him through this journey, and he couldn't help but feel immense appreciation for her support.

"Suraj, your poems were incredible! I felt every word," one friend exclaimed, pulling him into a hug.

"Thank you! That means so much to me," Suraj replied, his heart swelling with joy.

As the evening progressed, he signed copies of his book, each inscription a small token of his gratitude for those who had come to support him. It felt surreal, holding his published collection in his hands—a physical manifestation of his growth and resilience.

Later, Suraj found a quiet moment on the gallery's balcony, overlooking the city lights. The vibrant colors and bustling streets below mirrored the excitement swirling inside him. As he leaned against the railing, Maya joined him, a glass of sparkling juice in hand.

"You did it, Suraj! I'm so proud of you," she said, her eyes shining brightly.

"I couldn't have done it without you. You've been my rock throughout this whole process," he replied, turning to face her, his heart racing.

Maya smiled, her gaze softening. "I believe in your talent, Suraj. You have a gift for touching hearts with your words."

In that moment, something shifted between them—a connection deepening beyond friendship. Suraj felt a rush of emotions, a pull towards Maya that he had been hesitant to acknowledge before.

"Maya, I—" he started, his voice faltering as vulnerability washed over him.

Before he could finish, Maya reached out, placing a finger gently over his lips. "Suraj, I feel it too. There's something special here, something worth exploring."

Suraj's heart raced, and he felt a warmth spread through him. He leaned in closer, their faces mere inches apart. "Then let's explore it together," he whispered, his voice barely audible above the hum of the city below.

As their lips met, Suraj felt a spark ignite within him—a beautiful new beginning that felt as liberating as his journey through heartbreak. The kiss was tender and sweet, a promise of what was to come.

When they pulled away, Suraj looked into Maya's eyes, both of them smiling with the same realization: they were ready to embark on this new adventure together.

As they returned to the gallery, hand in hand, Suraj felt a profound sense of gratitude for the journey he had traveled.

His heart, once heavy with loss, was now open and ready to embrace the love that awaited him.

"The Launch," Suraj prepares for a pivotal moment in his journey: the release of his poetry collection, "From Heartbreak to Healing: A Poet's Journey."

As the chapter unfolds:

Preparation and Anticipation: Suraj experiences a whirlwind of emotions leading up to the launch event. With Maya's support, he meticulously organizes every detail, from selecting poems to creating promotional materials. Their bond strengthens as they work together, blending their creative energies.

The Event: The launch takes place in a vibrant art gallery adorned with fairy lights and filled with friends and family. Suraj reads heartfelt poems, sharing his journey of love and loss. The audience's warmth and encouragement validate his efforts, and he feels a sense of acceptance and connection.

A Moment of Clarity: After the reading, Suraj enjoys mingling with guests and signing copies of his book. In a quiet moment on the balcony with Maya, he acknowledges the feelings that have been growing between them. Their first kiss marks a turning point, symbolizing a new chapter filled with possibility.

This chapter highlights Suraj's transformation as he embraces his artistic aspirations while exploring a budding romance with Maya, showcasing themes of growth, vulnerability, and the beauty of new

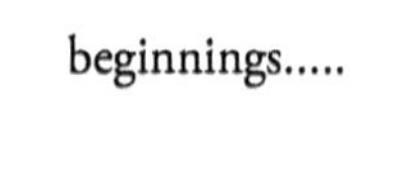
beginnings.....

15. New Beginnings

The weeks following the launch of "From Heartbreak to Healing: A Poet's Journey" were a blur of excitement and newfound joy for Suraj. His poetry collection had received positive feedback, and he found himself engaging more deeply in the literary community. Each day felt like a fresh start, filled with opportunities for growth, connection, and creativity.

Suraj and Maya's relationship blossomed in this new phase. They spent evenings at cozy cafés, sharing their dreams and passions over steaming cups of coffee. Their conversations flowed effortlessly, ranging from their favourite books to their aspirations for the future. Suraj found a deep sense of comfort in Maya's presence, something he had yearned for since his heartbreak with Parvati.

One rainy afternoon, they sat in a small coffee shop, the sound of raindrops tapping against the window providing a soothing backdrop to their laughter. Suraj looked across the table, watching as Maya animatedly spoke about her plans for a community art project. The way her eyes sparkled with enthusiasm made his heart swell.

"Maya, you should totally pursue this project," he encouraged, his voice warm with admiration. "You have a gift for bringing people together. It would be amazing to see your vision come to life."

Maya's cheeks flushed at the compliment. "You really think so? I've always wanted to create a space where people can express themselves artistically," she replied, her fingers fiddling with the edge of her coffee cup. "But I'm not sure if I have what it takes."

"You absolutely do. Just look at how you've helped me through my launch! You have this incredible ability to inspire others," he said, reaching across the table to gently touch her hand. "I believe in you."

Maya's smile widened, and in that moment, Suraj felt a connection that went beyond friendship—a bond built on mutual support and encouragement. As they finished their coffee, Suraj couldn't help but reflect on how much he had grown since the launch. The scars from his past were still there, but they no longer defined him. Instead, they served as reminders of his journey towards healing.

The following weekend, Suraj joined Maya at a local art fair, where she showcased her community project. The event was filled with vibrant displays of creativity, and Suraj felt inspired by the energy around him. As he walked alongside Maya, he observed how effortlessly she engaged with others, her passion lighting up the space.

"Let's gather some feedback on your project," he suggested, eager to support her efforts.

Maya's eyes lit up, and she nodded. "That would be great! I want to know how people respond to it."

As they approached a group of attendees, Suraj watched Maya confidently explain her vision. She spoke about creating a collaborative mural that would allow community members to contribute their artwork and express their stories. Suraj felt a surge of pride as he saw her come alive in her element.

After the presentation, Suraj and Maya took a break under a large oak tree, the sunlight filtering through the leaves above. They found a quiet moment away from the crowd, and Suraj couldn't help but admire how genuine Maya was—her kindness, her passion, and the way she brought light into the lives of those around her.

"Maya, I'm really proud of you. You have such a way with people," he said, sincerity coloring his tone.

"Thank you, Suraj. That means a lot coming from you," she replied, her voice soft. "You've inspired me too. Seeing you embrace your poetry has motivated me to pursue my dreams more seriously."

As they sat together, Suraj felt an overwhelming sense of gratitude for this new chapter in his life. He realised how healing it was to share his journey with someone who understood the value of vulnerability and growth. It was in this realization that he acknowledged a deeper truth—he was falling in love with Maya.

That night, as they walked back to Maya's apartment, the streets alive with laughter and chatter, Suraj felt a flutter of anticipation in his chest. The air was crisp, and the stars twinkled overhead, mirroring the excitement swirling within him.

"Hey, can I ask you something?" Suraj ventured, his voice slightly hesitant.

"Of course! What's on your mind?" Maya turned to face him, her expression open and encouraging.

"I've been thinking a lot about us and where we're headed. I just wanted to let you know how much I appreciate you in my life. You've become so important to me," he confessed, his heart racing.

Maya's eyes softened, and she stepped closer, her warmth radiating toward him. "Suraj, I feel the same way. I've really enjoyed our time together. It's been refreshing to explore this connection."

With her words, Suraj felt a rush of relief and happiness. "So, what do you think? Are you open to taking this to the next level? I'd love to explore a relationship with you, if you're interested," he asked, his voice steady despite the vulnerability of the moment.

Maya smiled, her eyes sparkling in the dim light. "I would love that, Suraj. I've been hoping we could see where this leads us."

As they exchanged shy smiles, Suraj took a step closer, feeling the undeniable pull between them. In that moment, he understood that healing didn't mean forgetting the past; it meant embracing new experiences and allowing oneself to be open to love again.

They shared a soft kiss under the glow of the streetlights, sealing the promise of this new beginning. Suraj felt as though the weight of his past was lifting, replaced by the excitement of what lay ahead.

16. The Dance of New Love

With the sweet taste of new love lingering in the air, Suraj and Maya settled into a comfortable rhythm. Their days were filled with laughter, deep conversations, and shared dreams. Suraj found himself writing more than ever, his poetry infused with the joy and hope that came from being with someone who understood him.

Maya's art project flourished, and Suraj often joined her in brainstorming sessions. They spent countless evenings discussing color palettes and designs, and each shared idea felt like a stroke of inspiration for both of them. Suraj was amazed at how seamlessly they complemented each other's creativity.

One afternoon, as they sat in Maya's cozy living room surrounded by sketches and paint swatches, Suraj noticed a glimmer of doubt in her eyes.

"Maya, is everything okay?" he asked gently, sensing her hesitation.

Maya sighed, pushing a strand of hair behind her ear. "I'm just feeling a bit overwhelmed with the project. There's so much pressure to make it perfect, and sometimes I wonder if I'm good enough to pull this off," she admitted, vulnerability creeping into her voice.

Suraj reached out, taking her hand in his. "You are more than good enough. You've already inspired so many people, including me. Remember that art isn't about perfection; it's about expression. Just be true to yourself, and everything will fall into place," he encouraged, squeezing her hand reassuringly.

Maya smiled softly, gratitude shining in her eyes. "Thank you, Suraj. I don't know what I'd do without your support."

"Let's take a break," Suraj suggested, wanting to lighten the mood. "How about we go for a walk? The weather's too nice to be cooped up inside."

Maya agreed, and they strolled through the nearby park, the sun casting a warm glow on the vibrant autumn leaves. Suraj felt invigorated by the fresh air and the lively atmosphere around them. He loved these moments spent together, where time seemed to stand still, allowing them to connect on a deeper level.

As they walked, Suraj pulled out a small notebook from his bag. "I've been writing some new poems, and I'd love to share them with you," he said, a mix of excitement and nervousness bubbling within him.

"Oh, I'd love that!" Maya replied enthusiastically. They found a quiet bench beneath a sprawling tree, and Suraj opened his notebook.

He read aloud a poem he had written about their blossoming relationship, capturing the beauty of their connection and the feelings of hope and warmth that had begun to fill his heart again:

"In Your Light"

"In your light, I see my way,

A gentle dawn, the start of day.

With every laugh, every shared glance,

You pull me closer into this dance.

No shadows loom, no doubts remain,

Just a symphony of joy, no pain.

In the rhythm of our hearts, we sway,

Two souls united, come what may."

As he finished reading, he glanced at Maya, whose eyes shimmered with emotion. "Suraj, that was beautiful! You have a way of capturing feelings that's truly magical," she said, her voice soft and filled with admiration.

Suraj felt a rush of warmth at her praise. "I'm glad you liked it. Writing about us has helped me process everything I've been through. It's like each poem is a step toward healing," he explained, the truth resonating deeply within him.

Maya leaned in closer, resting her head against his shoulder. "You've come so far, Suraj. I admire your strength and vulnerability. It's inspiring to see how you've channeled your pain into something so beautiful."

The sun began to dip below the horizon, casting a golden hue over the park. Suraj felt a deep sense of gratitude wash over him as they sat together, wrapped in each other's presence.

Days turned into weeks, and their bond deepened. They often collaborated on creative projects, merging their talents and inspiring one another in ways neither had anticipated. Suraj began to explore themes of love and healing in his poetry, weaving together his experiences with Maya's insights into art. However, the undercurrents of anxiety remained. Suraj couldn't shake the fear that lingered in the back of his mind—the fear of opening himself up completely and being hurt again. Parvati's betrayal still echoed in his heart, reminding him of the fragility of love.

One evening, as they prepared for a small art exhibition featuring Maya's community project, Suraj's anxiety bubbled to the surface. The event promised to draw a significant crowd, and the thought of it unnerved him. He couldn't help but wonder what would happen if things didn't go as planned or if he accidentally slipped back into old patterns of doubt.

"Maya," he began, his voice wavering slightly, "I want to be honest with you about something."

"Of course, what's on your mind?" she replied, her gaze attentive and encouraging.

"I've really enjoyed our time together, but sometimes I feel this nagging fear that I'm going to mess things up. I don't want to lose what we have, and I'm scared of getting hurt again," he confessed, his vulnerability palpable.

Maya's expression softened as she moved closer to him. "Suraj, it's natural to feel that way, especially after everything you've been through. But I want you to know that I'm here for you. We're in this together, and I believe in us," she reassured him.

Her words were like a balm to his soul, and he felt a wave of relief wash over him. "Thank you for being so understanding. I just want to be the best partner for you," he said, his heart swelling with appreciation.

"You already are," she replied, her smile brightening the moment. "Let's take it one step at a time, and remember that we're building something beautiful together."

As they stood in the soft glow of the evening light, Suraj felt a renewed sense of hope. He realised that love required courage and that facing fears together only strengthened their bond. The journey ahead would undoubtedly have its challenges, but with Maya by his side, he felt ready to embrace whatever came next.

17. The Art of Connection

The day of the art exhibition arrived, and the air buzzed with excitement. Suraj and Maya arrived early at the community center, where colorful banners hung and the scent of fresh paint lingered. The space was filled with art pieces from various local artists, but Maya's community project—a collaborative mural depicting stories of love, healing, and resilience—was the centrepiece of the exhibition.

As they set up the display, Suraj felt a mix of pride and anxiety. He admired Maya's hard work and the way she had brought the community together, yet the thought of people's reactions made his heart race.

"Maya, everything looks incredible," Suraj said, stepping back to take it all in. The mural, a vibrant explosion of colors and emotions, showcased contributions from various community members, each section telling a unique story. "You've created something truly special here."

Maya beamed, her face glowing with happiness. "Thank you, Suraj! I couldn't have done it without your support. It means so much to me that you're here."

As guests began to arrive, the atmosphere filled with laughter and chatter. Suraj watched as people marveled at the mural, sharing their thoughts and emotions inspired by the artwork.

He felt a sense of belonging, knowing that they were all part of something meaningful.

Maya moved among the guests, engaging them in conversations about the mural and the stories behind each piece. Suraj, standing off to the side, admired her confidence and ability to connect with others. He felt a surge of affection, realizing how much he admired her passion and dedication.

But as the crowd grew, Suraj's anxiety began to resurface. He noticed a familiar face in the crowd—Parvati. His heart raced at the sight of her, a mix of emotions swirling within him. He hadn't seen her since their breakup, and the memories flooded back, threatening to overshadow the joy of the day.

"Maya, I think Parvati is here," Suraj whispered, his voice laced with tension.

Maya looked over, her expression shifting to one of concern. "Are you okay? Do you want to talk to her?"

"No, I don't think so. I just… I'm not sure how I feel about seeing her," Suraj admitted, his heart pounding.

"Let's focus on the exhibition and having a good time," Maya encouraged, placing her hand on his arm. "You've worked hard for this. Don't let her take away from the celebration."

Taking a deep breath, Suraj nodded, trying to push aside the memories of his past. He wanted to be present for Maya and celebrate her achievements. He was determined not to let Parvati's presence ruin this moment.

As the evening progressed, Suraj engaged with the guests, sharing his own thoughts about the mural. He was amazed by how quickly he was able to connect with others, fueled by Maya's enthusiasm. The laughter and camaraderie enveloped him, momentarily drowning out his anxiety.

However, Parvati's presence loomed in the back of his mind. He saw her chatting with some mutual friends, her laughter ringing through the air, reminding him of the good times they once shared. He felt a pang of nostalgia but quickly reminded himself of the pain she had caused.

Just as he began to feel at ease, Suraj caught sight of Parvati walking toward him, a confident smile on her face. His heart sank.

"Suraj," she greeted, her tone light yet carrying an undertone of uncertainty. "It's good to see you here."

"Parvati," he replied, keeping his voice steady. "I didn't expect to see you."

"I wanted to check out the exhibition. I heard about your poetry launch, and I thought it would be nice to support," she said, her eyes scanning the mural.

Suraj felt a surge of conflicting emotions—anger, sadness, and lingering affection. "Well, it's great to see you," he said, trying to keep the conversation polite.

"I see you've been busy," Parvati continued, her gaze lingering on the mural. "This is really impressive. You both have done a wonderful job."

Before Suraj could respond, Maya approached, her warmth radiating through the tension-filled air. "Hi! I'm Maya, Suraj's friend and collaborator on this project," she introduced herself, extending her hand with a friendly smile.

Parvati's demeanor shifted slightly, her eyes narrowing as she regarded Maya. "Nice to meet you," she said, her tone cool.

"Maya and I have been working together to bring this mural to life," Suraj added, trying to ease the tension. "It's all about sharing stories and connecting through art."

"Sounds meaningful," Parvati replied, her voice devoid of warmth. Suraj sensed the underlying competition in her tone and felt protective of Maya.

"Would you like to contribute a story or artwork?" Maya offered, her voice cheerful and welcoming.

Suraj held his breath, hoping that Parvati would decline. But instead, she smiled—a sharp, knowing smile that sent a chill down Suraj's spine. "I might have something to share," she replied, her eyes gleaming with a hint of mischief.

Suraj's heart sank. He remembered the way Parvati had pulled away from their shared dreams, the way she had broken his heart. He didn't want her involvement to overshadow the love and creativity he had found with Maya.

As the conversation continued, Suraj felt increasingly anxious. He could see the tension building between Maya and Parvati, their contrasting energies clashing like opposing forces. He stepped closer to Maya, wanting to shield her from Parvati's indifference.

"Let's take a moment to appreciate the people who made this possible," Suraj suggested, trying to divert the focus back to the exhibition. "The stories shared in the mural are from our community, and we're grateful for everyone's contributions."

As he spoke, Suraj felt a sense of purpose wash over him. He was no longer the heartbroken poet dwelling on the past; he was a part of something beautiful and healing, a testament to the power of connection and creativity.

After a few moments, the attention shifted away from Parvati, and Suraj breathed a sigh of relief. He turned to Maya, who was looking at him with concern.

"Are you okay?" she asked softly, her eyes searching his.

"I'm fine," he assured her, though the unease lingered. "Let's focus on the art and the people who appreciate it."

The exhibition continued, filled with laughter and creativity. Suraj found himself enveloped in the joy of the evening, but the shadow of Parvati remained. He knew he had to confront his feelings once and for all.

As the night wore on, Suraj took Maya's hand, leading her away from the crowd to a quieter corner of the exhibition.

"Maya, can we talk for a moment?" he asked, his voice low.

"Of course," she replied, concern etched on her face.

Once they were away from the noise, Suraj took a deep breath. "I need to be honest with you. Seeing Parvati tonight has brought back a lot of feelings—ones I thought I had dealt with. I don't want that to affect us."

Maya nodded, her expression softening. "Suraj, it's okay to feel that way. You've been through a lot. Just remember that I'm here for you, and we can talk about it whenever you need."

Suraj smiled, grateful for her understanding. "I want you to know that what we have is important to me. I don't want the past to overshadow our present."

Maya squeezed his hand, her eyes filled with warmth. "We'll navigate this together. I'm not going anywhere," she reassured him.

As they stood together, the sounds of the exhibition fading into the background, Suraj realized that he had the power to define his future. With Maya by his side, he could face the ghosts of his past, no matter how daunting they might seem.

18. Preview: Closure

Suraj finds himself grappling with the need for closure regarding his relationship with Parvati. After the art exhibition, where emotions ran high, he realises that to fully embrace his future with Maya, he must confront his past. Suraj makes the decision to reach out to Parvati one last time, hoping to have an honest conversation that could bring him the peace he desperately seeks.

As he prepares for the meeting, Suraj reflects on how much he has grown since their breakup and the lessons he has learned about love, heartbreak, and healing. The chapter will delve into Suraj's emotional journey as he navigates his feelings and confronts Parvati.

During their meeting, Suraj expresses his feelings, seeking clarity on their relationship and understanding what went wrong. Parvati reveals her own struggles and insecurities, offering insights that Suraj never expected. Their conversation becomes a turning point, allowing Suraj to let go of past hurt and reclaim his sense of self.

By the end of the chapter, Suraj feels a weight lifted from his shoulders, ready to embrace the love and happiness that awaits him with Maya. The chapter emphasizes the importance of closure for personal growth and the power of honest communication in moving forward.

The following day, Suraj sat at his desk, his fingers hovering over the keyboard. He'd been mulling over his decision to reach out to Parvati, and he felt a swirl of emotions—nervousness, anticipation, and a hint of dread. After reflecting on the tumultuous journey he'd taken since their breakup, he knew that confronting the past was the only way to fully embrace his future.

With a deep breath, he opened his messaging app and began to type a message to Parvati.

Hey, Parvati. Can we meet up? I think we need to talk.

Once he hit send, a wave of anxiety washed over him. He didn't know how she would respond or if she would even agree to meet. Moments felt like hours as he waited for a reply, but finally, the three dots appeared on the screen, and soon enough, she replied.

Sure. How about tomorrow at the café?

The next day, Suraj arrived at the café earlier than their scheduled time. The familiar aroma of coffee filled the air, but it couldn't soothe his nerves. He picked a cozy corner table, trying to focus on the menu as he waited for Parvati.

When she arrived, Suraj felt his heart race. She looked different—more put together yet somehow more distant. He could see traces of the girl he once loved, but they were overshadowed by the distance that had formed between them.

"Hi," she greeted, taking a seat across from him.

"Hi," he replied, forcing a smile. "Thanks for meeting me."

Parvati nodded, her expression unreadable. "What did you want to talk about?"

Suraj took a deep breath, trying to find the right words. "I wanted to talk about us. About what happened between us," he started, feeling the weight of the conversation hanging in the air. "I think we both deserve some closure."

Parvati sighed, leaning back in her chair. "I guess that makes sense. It was a messy breakup, and I've had a lot of time to think about it."

Suraj nodded, his heart pounding. "I've been working through a lot of emotions since then. I just want to understand why things went the way they did."

Parvati looked out the window for a moment, collecting her thoughts. "I think… I lost myself in the relationship. I was overwhelmed, and I didn't handle things well. I started talking to my ex because I thought I needed someone familiar, someone who understood me better than I thought you did."

Suraj felt a stab of pain at her words but reminded himself to listen. "I wish you had come to me instead of pulling away. I wanted to support you through whatever you were feeling."

"I know," she said, her voice softening. "But I was scared. I didn't know how to express what I was going through. It was easier to run away."

Suraj's mind raced with memories of their time together—the laughter, the dreams they had shared. "I think that's the hardest part for me. I loved you, and I wanted to be there for you. But instead, I felt like I lost you completely."

Parvati looked him in the eye, and for a moment, Suraj saw a flicker of the connection they once had. "I didn't want to hurt you. I thought breaking up would be easier for both of us, but it turned out to be so much more painful."

Suraj felt the tension in his chest start to ease. "I've had to process a lot of pain and confusion since we broke up. I've realised that I need to let go of that hurt to move forward."

"Me too," Parvati admitted, her eyes glistening with unshed tears. "It's been hard, and I've had to confront my own mistakes. I never wanted it to end this way."

"I know that now," Suraj said, feeling a sense of understanding wash over him. "I've learned that not every relationship is meant to last, and that's okay. But I needed to hear your side to find closure for myself."

Parvati nodded, wiping a tear from her cheek. "I'm really sorry for how things ended. I hope you can find happiness."

Suraj felt a weight lift from his shoulders. "Thank you. I appreciate that. I hope you find your peace too."

They shared a moment of silence, both processing the conversation. Suraj realised that this was the closure he had sought—an acknowledgment of their past and the acceptance of their separate futures.

"I want you to know that I've started seeing someone," Suraj said carefully. "Her name is Maya. She's been an incredible friend and has helped me heal."

Parvati's expression shifted slightly, but she managed a smile. "I'm glad to hear that. You deserve to be happy."

"Thank you. I hope you find someone who understands you too," he replied, feeling a sense of relief.

As they wrapped up their conversation, Suraj felt a newfound sense of clarity. He and Parvati shared one last smile, a silent agreement that they were ready to move on from the past. He stood to leave, feeling lighter than he had in months.

"Take care, Suraj," Parvati said softly, her voice sincere.

"You too," he replied, feeling the finality of their parting.

Stepping outside, Suraj took a deep breath, feeling the weight of the past lift from his shoulders. The sun shone brightly overhead, and he could feel a new chapter beginning to unfold. He had confronted his feelings, faced the pain, and now he was free to embrace the love that awaited him with Maya.

As he walked away from the café, he felt a renewed sense of hope. Suraj had found closure, and in doing so, he had reclaimed his heart.

19. A New Beginning

Suraj walked through the park, the sun dipping lower in the sky, casting a golden hue over everything. The fresh air filled his lungs, and with each step, he felt lighter. The conversation with Parvati had been cathartic, allowing him to release the lingering emotions he had held onto for too long. Now, he was ready to fully embrace his new beginning.

As he arrived at his favourite bench overlooking the small lake, he sat down and took out his notebook. The urge to write had been strong since his meeting with Parvati. He flipped to a fresh page and let his thoughts flow.

The weight of the past has lifted,

From shadows, I've finally drifted.

With every word, I shed the pain,

In sunlight's warmth, I bloom again.

He paused, considering the change in his heart. Suraj felt an unexpected thrill as he thought of Maya. Their friendship had blossomed into something beautiful and promising, and he couldn't wait to see where it would lead.

The next day, Suraj met Maya at their favourite coffee shop. The warm ambiance was filled with the scent of freshly brewed coffee and pastries, and he felt an instant sense of comfort as he spotted her at a corner table, engrossed in a book.

"Hey!" he greeted, his smile wide.

Maya looked up, her face lighting up at his presence. "Hi! I was just thinking about you. How did it go with Parvati?"

Suraj settled into the seat across from her. "It went well. I finally got the closure I needed. We talked about everything, and I feel so much lighter now."

Maya's eyes sparkled with interest. "That's great to hear! I knew you needed that. How do you feel about moving forward?"

Suraj leaned in, feeling a rush of excitement. "I'm ready. I think I can fully embrace what's happening between us now."

He felt a sense of liberation as he said the words, realizing how genuine his feelings for her had become.

Maya's cheeks flushed slightly. "I'm glad to hear that. I really like where this is going."

Their conversation flowed effortlessly, laughter punctuating their words as they shared stories and dreams. Suraj found himself captivated by her passion and the ease of their connection. The more they talked, the more he recognised that he had finally begun to move on.

As they finished their coffees, Suraj felt a surge of confidence. "Maya, can I ask you something?"

"Of course!" she replied, her eyes curious.

"I know we've been getting to know each other better, but would you like to go on a proper date with me? Just us?" he asked, holding his breath in anticipation.

Maya's expression softened, and she nodded. "I would love that!"

A wave of relief washed over him, and he couldn't help but grin. They spent the next hour planning their date, excitement bubbling between them as they exchanged ideas for a picnic in the park.

That evening, Suraj returned home, feeling an unfamiliar sense of joy. He sat down with his notebook once more, eager to capture this new chapter in his life.

In blooming gardens, love will grow,

A chance to shine, a chance to glow.

With you beside me, I feel so free,

In every moment, just you and me.

As he penned down his thoughts, he realised that the pain from his past had transformed into something beautiful—an understanding of love and loss that enriched his life.

The following weekend, Suraj and Maya met for their picnic. He arrived at the park with a basket filled with homemade sandwiches, fresh fruits, and a couple of sweet treats. The sun shone brightly, and a gentle breeze rustled the leaves around them.

Maya was already waiting, her smile radiant as she spotted him approaching. "This looks amazing!" she exclaimed, eyeing the basket eagerly.

"I hope you're hungry," Suraj replied, setting it down on a blanket spread out beneath a large oak tree.

They settled onto the blanket, sharing food and laughter. With each passing moment, Suraj felt the warmth of connection growing stronger. Their conversations ranged from light-hearted banter to deeper discussions about their dreams and aspirations.

As the afternoon wore on, they lay back on the blanket, staring up at the clouds drifting lazily by. Suraj turned his head to Maya, feeling a flutter in his chest. "You know, I didn't expect to feel this way so soon. It's refreshing," he admitted.

Maya looked over at him, her eyes sparkling. "I feel the same. It's like we just click, you know?"

Suraj nodded, his heart swelling with affection. "I'm glad we took the leap to explore this together."

Suddenly, Maya sat up, a playful glint in her eye. "Let's play a game! How about we share our most embarrassing moments?"

Suraj laughed, the idea lighting up the mood. "Oh, I have a few stories that might make you cringe!"

As they shared their stories, Suraj felt the walls he had built around his heart begin to crumble. With Maya, he could be himself—open and vulnerable. Each laugh, each shared secret drew them closer, and he couldn't help but think that this was where he was meant to be.

The sun began to set, casting a warm glow over the park as they finished their picnic. Suraj turned to Maya, feeling a sense of urgency. "Can I tell you something?"

"Of course," she replied, her voice steady.

"I've been through a lot, and I thought I'd never find someone who could make me feel whole again. But with you, everything feels different. I feel alive," he confessed, searching her eyes for a reaction.

Maya's expression softened, and she reached for his hand. "I feel the same way, Suraj. You've brought so much joy into my life, and I'm really excited about what's to come."

Suraj's heart raced at her words. In that moment, he realised he had opened his heart once again. The shadows of his past had faded, replaced by the warmth of new love. As the sun dipped below the horizon, Suraj leaned closer to Maya, feeling an undeniable urge to kiss her.

He brushed his lips against hers gently, savouring the sweetness of the moment. Maya responded, her kiss warm and inviting. Suraj closed his eyes, feeling a rush of emotions—relief, happiness, and a deep sense of belonging.

As they pulled away, he knew that this was just the beginning. Together, they would navigate the path ahead, hand in hand, ready to embrace whatever life had in store for them.

20. Navigating New Waters

Suraj awoke the next morning feeling a sense of peace he hadn't experienced in a long time. Sunlight filtered through his window, illuminating the room in a warm glow. He rolled over, reaching for his notebook on the bedside table, the one that had become a sanctuary for his thoughts and emotions.

As he scribbled down ideas for his next poem, the events of the previous day flooded his mind. Maya. The name brought a smile to his face. After their magical picnic and first kiss, he felt as if he were on the brink of something beautiful.

That week, Suraj and Maya spent more time together. They explored different cafés, attended open mic nights, and visited art galleries, each outing deepening their connection. Suraj found himself enthralled not only by her laughter and warmth but also by her passion for art. She shared stories about her favourite painters and how art had always been a significant part of her life.

On a rainy Thursday, they found themselves in a cozy café, sipping hot chocolate and watching raindrops race down the window. Suraj felt a sudden burst of inspiration and pulled out his notebook. "Can I share a poem with you?" he asked, his heart pounding with excitement.

"Absolutely!" Maya replied, her eyes bright with curiosity.

He cleared his throat and read aloud:

In the dance of rain, we find our tune,

With every drop, our hearts commune.

Two souls entwined in a world so wide,

With you, I'm home, with you, I'll abide.

As he finished, he looked up to see Maya's eyes glistening with emotion. "That was beautiful, Suraj. You have such a way with words."

Suraj felt a flush of warmth at her praise. "Thank you. Writing helps me express everything I sometimes struggle to say out loud."

Maya leaned forward, her expression serious yet gentle. "You know, I want to share something with you, too."

Suraj's heart raced as he nodded, eager to hear what she had to say.

"I've always been afraid to let people in," she confessed. "I've had my share of heartbreaks, and it's been hard for me to trust. But with you, it feels different. I'm learning to let go of those fears."

Suraj felt a surge of empathy for her. "I understand. I was stuck in that same place for a long time. But I think we're both ready for this."

Maya smiled, a mixture of relief and joy on her face. "Yes, let's embrace it together."

Days turned into weeks, and their relationship continued to blossom. Suraj found joy in the little moments they shared, from laughing over silly inside jokes to exploring new corners of the city. Each date felt like a new adventure, and every moment spent together solidified the bond they were forming.

Yet, as much as Suraj revealed in his new love, he occasionally caught himself thinking of the past. He realised he hadn't fully confronted the impact of his previous relationship with Parvati, and he didn't want that to overshadow the happiness he had with Maya.

One evening, while sitting on a park bench beneath the stars, Suraj decided to bring it up. "Maya," he began, his voice steady but gentle, "can we talk about our pasts? I think it's important for us."

Maya looked at him thoughtfully. "Of course. I think it's good to share those things."

"I've been thinking about my relationship with Parvati," Suraj admitted. "It was intense and beautiful at first, but it ended in pain and confusion. I just want you to know that I'm working on healing from that. You deserve to know where I'm coming from."

Maya nodded, her eyes soft with understanding. "Thank you for sharing that with me. I want you to know that I have my own scars from past relationships. It's not easy to open up, but I believe in us."

Suraj felt a sense of relief wash over him. Sharing their vulnerabilities allowed them to connect on a deeper level, reinforcing the foundation of trust they were building.

As they sat beneath the stars, Suraj felt a surge of gratitude for Maya and the journey they were on together. He was beginning to understand that love didn't mean forgetting the past; it meant growing from it and allowing it to shape a brighter future.

Over the next few months, Suraj found himself inspired to write more than ever. Each poem became a reflection of his evolving feelings for Maya, and he even began to submit some of his work to local poetry competitions.

One day, he received an email confirming that he had been selected to perform at an upcoming poetry slam. Excited yet nervous, he shared the news with Maya over dinner.

"I'm so proud of you!" she exclaimed, her eyes sparkling with enthusiasm. "You're going to be amazing. I can't wait to see you perform!"

"Will you come?" Suraj asked, his voice tinged with hope.

"Absolutely! I wouldn't miss it for the world," she replied, reaching across the table to squeeze his hand.

The night of the poetry slam arrived, and Suraj felt a whirlwind of emotions as he prepared backstage. Maya's presence in the audience provided him with an extra boost of confidence. He took a deep breath, visualising the supportive smile she would give him when he stepped onto the stage.

As he took his place in front of the microphone, the crowd fell silent. Suraj's heart raced, but he reminded himself that he was not just sharing his poetry; he was sharing his journey, and that was something he could be proud of.

He began to speak, each word flowing effortlessly from his heart. The energy in the room surged as he recited his poems, the audience captivated by the raw emotion and vulnerability he shared.

When he finished, the applause erupted, echoing around him like a warm embrace. Suraj scanned the crowd, his eyes landing on Maya. Her face beamed with pride, and he felt an overwhelming rush of gratitude.

After the performance, Maya rushed up to him, her excitement contagious. "You were incredible! I knew you could do it!"

"Thanks! I can't believe I just did that," Suraj replied, still riding the high of the moment.

Maya took his hand, pulling him into a warm embrace. "You've come so far, Suraj. I'm so glad I got to witness this."

As they stood there, wrapped in each other's warmth, Suraj realised how far he had come—not just in his poetry but in his heart. He was learning to embrace love again, and with Maya by his side, the future felt brighter than ever.

21. A New Horizon

Suraj's poetry performance marked a pivotal moment in his journey. That night wasn't just about sharing his words with an audience; it was about reclaiming his voice and rediscovering his purpose after months of heartache. The applause from the crowd felt like a release, not just for him, but for everything he had carried since the breakup with Parvati.

In the days that followed, he noticed a shift within himself. His poems, once saturated with longing and grief, now carried traces of hope and healing. Delhi's bustling streets and crowded cafés became his playground for inspiration, with each corner sparking new ideas and emotions. And in the crowd that night, Maya had been there, offering her silent support. The bond between them was undeniable, and their connection deepened with every passing moment.

Suraj's life in Greater Noida felt far removed from the chaos of Delhi, but it offered a peaceful retreat after long days of work and poetry readings in the capital. He loved the contrast: the quiet nights in Greater Noida, with its sprawling roads and open spaces, and the vibrant, buzzing energy of Delhi. On weekends, Maya would often visit him, and they'd spend hours talking on his balcony, watching the distant lights of the city flicker.

One particular Saturday, after a long day of exploring the narrow lanes of Old Delhi and sampling chaat from Chandni Chowk, they found themselves sitting by the Yamuna River. The golden hues of the setting sun reflected on the water as they shared a comfortable silence, interrupted only by the occasional honk of distant traffic.

As they watched the world go by, Maya turned to Suraj with a thoughtful expression. "Suraj, I've been thinking a lot lately."

Suraj shifted his gaze from the river to her. "About what?"

Maya hesitated for a moment, choosing her words carefully. "About us. About where we're headed."

Suraj felt his heart skip a beat. While their relationship had blossomed over the past few months, they hadn't really discussed their future. They were content in their little bubble, floating between Greater Noida's calm and Delhi's vibrant pulse.

"I've been thinking about it too," Suraj finally said. "I care about you, Maya. A lot. I don't have all the answers right now, but I know I want you to be a part of my life."

Maya smiled, a small, genuine smile that lit up her face. "That's what I needed to hear. I don't need a plan. I just need to know we're on the same page."

They sat together, hands intertwined, watching the sun dip below the horizon. The future still felt uncertain, but in that moment, it didn't matter. They were building something together, step by step.

As Suraj's poetry gained popularity in Delhi's literary circles, life seemed to move at an exciting pace. He was invited to perform at several cafés in South Delhi—places like Hauz Khas Village and Khan Market, where the crowd was both discerning and passionate. Maya never missed a performance. She cheered for him from the sidelines, her support unwavering. He even began working on compiling his poetry into a collection, something Maya was more than willing to help with.

They found joy in the simplest things—long drives back to Greater Noida, sipping chai from roadside stalls near India Gate, and discussing life while strolling through the gardens of Qutub Minar. Everything felt like it was falling into place, and Suraj often marveled at how far he had come from the heartbreak that had once consumed him.

But life, as always, had a way of throwing the unexpected.

One evening, after another successful performance at a quaint café in Connaught Place, they returned to Suraj's apartment in Greater Noida. As they settled onto his balcony, the quiet of the night surrounding them, Maya's expression changed. Her usual warmth was tinged with hesitation.

"Suraj, there's something I need to tell you," she said softly.

Suraj, sensing her seriousness, turned to her with concern. "What is it?"

Maya looked down at her hands before meeting his eyes. "I've been offered a job…in Mumbai."

The words hit Suraj like a punch to the gut. Mumbai—so far from Delhi, from their weekend explorations and quiet nights in Greater Noida. His mind raced as he tried to process what this meant for them.

"Mumbai?" he repeated, his voice betraying his shock. "That's…that's amazing, Maya. It's such a great opportunity."

Maya nodded, but her smile was faint. "It is. But it also means things will change. A lot."

Suraj felt the weight of her words. He didn't want to hold her back from this incredible opportunity, but the thought of her leaving Delhi, leaving him, filled him with a sadness he hadn't anticipated.

"I don't want you to give this up," he said finally, though his heart ached as he spoke. "You've worked so hard for this, and you deserve it. But…what about us?"

Maya's eyes softened as she reached out to hold his hand. "I don't know what this means for us, Suraj. But I don't want to lose what we have. Maybe we can make it work, even with the distance."

Suraj squeezed her hand, his voice firm despite the turmoil inside him. "We'll figure it out. I don't want to lose you either."

The weeks leading up to Maya's departure were a whirlwind of emotions. They tried to make the most of their time together, visiting their favorite spots around Delhi and Greater Noida, creating memories they could hold onto. They talked about how they would manage the long distance—frequent visits, video calls, keeping their communication open.

But the reality of the distance weighed heavily on both of them. Suraj, who had once felt so secure in their relationship, now faced an uncertain future. Yet, despite his fears, he knew one thing: he didn't want to lose Maya.

The day of her departure arrived sooner than either of them expected. They stood together at the New Delhi railway station, the sound of train whistles and the hum of the crowd filling the air. Suraj held Maya close, the weight of the moment pressing down on him.

"This isn't goodbye," Maya whispered, her voice thick with emotion.

"I know," Suraj replied, though his heart felt heavy. "We'll make this work."

As Maya boarded the train, Suraj stood there, watching her until she disappeared from view. The ache in his chest was undeniable, but amidst the sadness, he felt a sense of resolve. This wasn't the end of their story—just a new chapter.

"The Path Ahead"

The city lights fade into the night,

And still, I hold you in my sight.

Though miles may stretch between our hands,

In love, we'll find where each heart stands.

The road ahead may twist and turn,

But for your touch, my heart will yearn.

No distance great, no time too long,

Together, in spirit, we'll stay strong.

22. The Distance Between Us

Suraj had always been someone who believed that love could overcome any obstacle. Yet, as the weeks passed after Maya's departure to Mumbai, he realised just how hard maintaining a long-distance relationship could be. The excitement of their first few phone calls and video chats soon gave way to missed messages, delayed replies, and conversations that felt strained. Life in Delhi continued, but there was a void in his routine. Every time he returned to his apartment in Greater Noida after a long day at work or a poetry reading, the silence felt more oppressive. He missed the easy companionship he shared with Maya—the laughter, the shared experiences, and most of all, her physical presence.

The poetry that had once flowed so easily now seemed forced. His words felt disconnected, much like his relationship with Maya. He tried to focus on the positives—Maya was thriving in her new job, and they were doing their best to stay in touch—but the emotional distance was growing.

One weekend, after another lonely evening, Suraj found himself scrolling through old pictures of him and Maya. There were photos of their trips to Old Delhi, their impromptu chai breaks, and the peaceful evenings they spent on his balcony in Greater Noida. The memories made his heart ache. It was hard to believe that their once-vibrant relationship was now reduced to fleeting phone calls and occasional text messages.

His phone buzzed, and he saw a message from Maya. It was a picture of the Mumbai skyline at night, accompanied by a message: "Wish you were here to see this."

Suraj stared at the message for a while before typing his reply: "I miss you too. Wish I was there with you." But even as he sent the message, a sense of helplessness washed over him. He couldn't be there, and the distance between them was becoming harder to bear.

In the following weeks, the time difference and their busy schedules began to take a toll. Suraj's poetry performances were becoming more frequent in Delhi, and Maya's new job demanded longer hours in Mumbai. Conversations became shorter, and the intimacy they once shared felt distant.

One evening, after a particularly exhausting day, Suraj sat on his balcony, looking out at the city lights of Greater Noida. His phone buzzed, and he saw a missed call from Maya. He immediately called her back, but there was no answer. After a few minutes, she texted him: "Hey, I'm so sorry, I've had a crazy day at work. Can we talk tomorrow?"

Suraj understood—he always did—but the disappointment lingered. "Sure, no problem. Get some rest," he replied, setting his phone aside.

The reality was sinking in: no matter how hard they tried, the distance was beginning to affect their relationship in ways they hadn't anticipated.

The following weekend, Suraj decided to surprise Maya with a visit. He booked a flight to Mumbai, hoping that the time together would rekindle the connection they once had. When he landed in Mumbai, the city's energy hit him immediately—the honking cars, the crowded streets, and the salty air from the Arabian Sea. It was so different from Delhi, yet vibrant in its own way.

He messaged Maya, "I'm in Mumbai. Surprise! Can't wait to see you."

Her response came a few minutes later: "Wow! You're here? That's amazing! But… I'm working late tonight, and I have a deadline tomorrow. I don't know if I'll have much time to spend with you this weekend."

Suraj's heart sank. He had imagined a weekend of catching up, exploring the city, and strengthening their bond. But it seemed like even this surprise visit wouldn't go as planned.

"It's okay. Maybe we can meet for dinner?" he suggested, trying to keep his disappointment in check.

"I'll try, but I can't promise anything," came Maya's reply.

That night, Suraj found himself sitting alone at a small café near Marine Drive, watching couples walk by hand in hand. The excitement of surprising Maya had faded, replaced by a sense of isolation. When Maya finally called, it was late, and she sounded exhausted.

"I'm so sorry, Suraj," she said over the phone. "I really wanted to spend time with you, but work has been insane."

"It's okay," Suraj said, trying to sound understanding, though the loneliness in his voice was evident. "I just wanted to see you."

"I know, and I appreciate you coming all the way here. Maybe next time we can plan something better."

"Yeah, maybe next time."

As Suraj walked along Marine Drive later that night, the waves crashing against the rocks, he couldn't help but wonder if their relationship was slowly slipping away. The distance was proving to be more than just physical. It was emotional too.

"The Miles Between Us"

The miles stretch far, a distant shore,

Yet I feel your heart no more.

The calls we share, the texts we send,

Feel like echoes that will never mend.

In crowded streets, I walk alone,

Wishing you were here, not on the phone.

Our love was bright, our days were sweet,

But now, it's just a memory's beat.

Suraj returned to Delhi the next day, disheartened. As his plane took off, he looked out of the window, watching Mumbai disappear into the clouds. He had come with the hope of reigniting their love, but the visit had only left him feeling more uncertain about the future.

Back in Greater Noida, life resumed its usual rhythm. He poured himself into his poetry and his work, but the distance between him and Maya weighed heavily on his mind. He wondered if love could truly survive when two people were living separate lives, miles apart.

23. Fading Echoes

Back in Greater Noida, Suraj tried to convince himself that things would get better. Long-distance relationships were difficult, yes, but love was supposed to withstand such trials, wasn't it? His heart, however, told a different story. The energy that once fueled their conversations was gone, and what remained was an unspoken tension. The more he tried to hold onto the relationship, the more distant Maya seemed.

One evening, while sitting on his balcony, the evening sky painted in hues of orange and pink, Suraj's thoughts drifted back to the early days with Maya. He missed her laughter, the small gestures of affection, and the way she looked at him like he was the only person that mattered.

Now, everything felt like an echo of something that used to be.

The phone rang, snapping him out of his thoughts. It was Maya.

"Hey," she said, her voice tired. "How was your day?"

"It was fine," Suraj replied, trying to keep his tone light. "How about you?"

"Same old," she sighed. "Work's been crazy."

There was a pause. Suraj wanted to say something—anything that could bridge the growing gap between them—but the words wouldn't come.

Instead, he asked, "When do you think you'll visit Delhi?"

"I don't know," Maya replied. "Work is just… it's a lot right now. I'll let you know when things calm down."

Another pause. The distance between them wasn't just physical—it was emotional, too.

"The Quiet Between Us"

Between our words, there's silence thick,

A quiet ache, a heavy brick.

The love we had, once loud and clear,

Now whispers faint, too hard to hear.

You speak of work, I speak of days,

But in our hearts, we've lost our ways.

The miles stretch far, but more than that,

It's in our hearts where we fall flat.

A week later, Suraj tried to plan a visit to Mumbai. He wanted to take control, to reignite what had been lost. He booked a ticket for the following weekend, determined to make things work. But two days before his trip, Maya called.

"I don't think this is a good idea, Suraj," she said softly. "I'm just… not sure where we're headed."

Her words felt like a punch to his gut. He had sensed the distance, of course, but hearing it from her made it real.

"What do you mean?" he asked, trying to keep his voice steady.

"I don't know if I can do this anymore. The distance, the pressure—it's all too much. I care about you, but I think we're just growing apart."

Suraj sat in stunned silence. His heart raced, his mind searching for the right thing to say, but all he could muster was, "Are you sure?"

"I think it's for the best," Maya replied, her voice barely above a whisper.

"Love Unspoken"

I tried to hold you, but you slipped away,

Like sand between my fingers, you wouldn't stay.

The words I feared, you spoke them true,

And now I stand, without a clue.

I loved you deep, I loved you whole,

But now I wander, a broken soul.

The distance wasn't just of land,

It was the heart, we didn't plan.

That night, Suraj sat on his balcony, staring at the night sky. He had poured so much of himself into their relationship, believing that love could conquer anything. But now, all that remained was a hollow space where his hope used to be.

Maya had been the first person he had truly opened up to. They had shared dreams, laughed over silly jokes, and made promises about the future. But in the end, reality had torn them apart.

As the night deepened, Suraj picked up his notebook and began writing. His heart ached, but the words flowed with a painful clarity.

"The Last Goodbye"

Goodbye, my love, we couldn't last,

Our love a dream, now in the past.

The miles between us too wide to cross,

Our love once bright, now it's our loss.

You were my heart, my light, my flame,

But now we part, no one to blame.

I'll keep our moments close, they'll stay,

But now it's time to walk away.

Days passed, and Suraj found himself reflecting on everything. Love, he realised, wasn't just about feelings—it was about timing, effort, and understanding. And sometimes, despite the best intentions, things just didn't work out.

Maya had meant the world to him, but holding on to something that was already gone wasn't fair to either of them. He needed to let go—not just for her, but for himself.

As he closed his notebook and set his pen down, Suraj felt a sense of closure. The relationship might have ended, but the love they shared had taught him invaluable lessons. He was stronger now, and even though it hurt, he knew he would heal.

24. Healing Wounds

As the weeks passed, Suraj began to embrace his solitude. The pain of losing Maya still lingered, but he knew it was part of the healing process. In the quiet moments, he reflected on everything their relationship had taught him—the joy, the challenges, the heartache. While it hadn't ended the way he'd hoped, it had shaped him in ways he couldn't yet fully understand.

Delhi's bustling energy surrounded him as he moved through his days. Greater Noida remained his sanctuary, a place where he could retreat from the world, but his heart felt lighter now. Each morning, he would wake up to the warmth of the rising sun, feeling a little less broken than the day before.

Suraj had thrown himself back into his poetry, attending open mics across Delhi, finding solace in the words he shared and the applause that followed. There was something therapeutic about standing in front of a crowd, pouring his heart into each line. It was as if every poem was a step toward mending the cracks in his heart.

One evening, Suraj attended a poetry event at Connaught Place. The venue was small, intimate, with soft lighting and quiet chatter in the background. As he sat at a table, waiting for his turn to perform, he felt an odd sense of peace. He was still healing, but the pain didn't consume him the way it once did.

When his name was called, he walked up to the mic, feeling a familiar rush of adrenaline. He looked at the faces in the crowd, strangers all, but somehow, they felt like a part of his journey.

"This one's called 'A Heart Rebuilt,'" he said into the microphone, his voice steady.

"A Heart Rebuilt"

I was shattered once, but now I mend,

Each broken piece, a lesson penned.

The love I lost, it taught me true,

That healing starts when I love me too.

Through storms I walked, through pain I bled,

But in the end, my heart was led.

To peace I found within my chest,

A love for self, the truest test.

No longer seeking from someone else,

I found my home within myself.

The audience clapped, and Suraj smiled, grateful for the way his words resonated. The applause wasn't just for the poem—it was for the journey he had survived. As he left the stage and took his seat, he felt lighter than he had in months. In the following days, Suraj found himself reconnecting with old friends and spending more time with his family. Life had a different rhythm now, one that wasn't centered around someone else but rather his own growth and well-being.

One afternoon, he visited the India Gate, a place that had always been a source of inspiration for him. Sitting on the grass, he pulled out his notebook and began to write. The words came easily, flowing from a place of acceptance and peace.

"The Gift of Letting Go"

To let you go was not a choice,

But a whisper from my inner voice.

I held on tight, I tried so hard,

But love, it faltered, left me scarred.

Yet now I see, in letting you fly,

I found the wings to soar, to try.

The world awaits, and so do I,

No longer bound, no longer shy.

For love begins within the soul,

And letting go has made me whole.

As Suraj finished writing, he looked up at the bustling city around him. Delhi, with its chaos and beauty, felt like a reflection of his own heart. It had been a tumultuous journey, but through it all, he had found a sense of inner peace.

The pain of his breakup with Maya hadn't disappeared, but it had transformed. It was no longer a wound, but a scar—a reminder of the love he once had and the strength he had found in its aftermath.

He knew now that healing wasn't about forgetting. It was about remembering the good, learning from the bad, and moving forward with the understanding that love—real love—begins within.

As the sun began to set, casting a golden glow over the India Gate, Suraj felt a quiet contentment settle over him. He didn't know what the future held, but for the first time in a long time, he wasn't afraid. He had survived heartbreak, and in doing so, he had found a deeper, more resilient version of himself.

And that, he realised, was the greatest love story of all.

25. Embracing the Unknown

The autumn air in Delhi was crisp, and the city was alive with the sights and sounds of a new season. The transition from summer to winter always brought with it a certain nostalgia for Suraj, but this year, it felt different. The weight of his past heartbreak had begun to lift, and now, as he walked through the streets of Connaught Place, he felt a strange sense of anticipation. Not for another relationship, but for what life had yet to offer him.

Suraj had immersed himself fully in the Delhi poetry scene, meeting new writers and artists who inspired him. The friendships he formed with fellow poets felt more meaningful than before. They understood the rawness that came from turning heartache into art, and that shared vulnerability created a bond he hadn't expected.

One evening, after an open mic at a small café in Hauz Khas Village, Suraj found himself in a deep conversation with Kavya, a fellow poet he had met a few months ago. Kavya's words had always resonated with him, and her presence had become something of a comfort in this new chapter of his life.

"I think heartbreak is the best muse for a poet," she said, sipping her tea. "But it's also a reminder of how resilient we are."

Suraj nodded, understanding the sentiment completely. "I used to think heartbreak was something to be avoided at all costs. But now, I see it as a kind of teacher."

Kavya smiled. "Exactly. It teaches us about love, about ourselves, and about the world."

Their conversation drifted to their favourite poets, and as they talked, Suraj realized how much he had changed. The person he was a year ago—the one who had been broken by Maya's absence—would never have believed he could sit here, speaking about love and loss without feeling the crushing weight of it.

"The Growth in Pain"

From pain, I learned to rise again,

Through tears, I found the sun in rain.

The love that broke me, set me free,

To find the strength inside of me.

I once believed the hurt would last,

But now it's just a shadowed past.

In every scar, a lesson lies,

And from the wounds, I learned to rise.

Days turned into weeks, and soon, Suraj felt as if he had truly moved on. Maya was still a part of his story, but she no longer defined it. He had grown from that experience, and now, he was ready for whatever came next.

One afternoon, as Suraj walked through the sprawling gardens of Lodhi Garden, notebook in hand, he realised how much he had come to love his own company. The peace he had once sought in others was now something he carried within himself. He sat beneath a tree, feeling the gentle breeze, and opened his notebook to a fresh page.

Without hesitation, he began to write.

"The Path Forward"

The road ahead is wide and clear,

No longer bound by love or fear.

I walk alone, yet not alone,

For in myself, I've found my home.

No longer searching for what's gone,

I move with strength, I carry on.

The past, it whispers, but it's light,

For in the dark, I've found my sight.

The future calls, I answer true,

With open heart, I welcome new.

As the sun dipped lower in the sky, casting long shadows across the grass, Suraj felt a sense of closure. He had survived the hardest part of his journey—losing someone he loved—and had come out the other side stronger, wiser, and more attuned to his own needs and desires.

That evening, back in Greater Noida, Suraj sat on his balcony, watching the city lights flicker in the distance. The skyline reminded him that life was always moving, always evolving, and so was he.

Suraj no longer felt the need to rush into the next chapter. He had learned to trust the process, to let things unfold in their own time. Whether love found him again or not, he knew he would be okay. For the first time, he felt complete—just as he was.

"Whole Again"

I once was broken, lost and weak,

But now I stand, no need to seek.

For in my heart, I've found the key,

To love myself, to just be me.

No longer searching for a part,

I've found the wholeness in my heart.

The love I sought, I've finally found,

Within myself, on solid ground.

The future calls, but I don't chase,

I welcome life with open grace.

26. A New Beginning

Months had passed since Suraj had let go of his past, and winter had come to Delhi. The air was cooler, crisp with the promise of new beginnings. Life in Greater Noida had settled into a rhythm that Suraj found both peaceful and fulfilling. He still attended poetry readings and events across the city, but there was a newfound calm in his heart, a quiet acceptance of life's unpredictability.

It was a Sunday afternoon when Suraj received an unexpected message from an old friend, Aditi, someone he hadn't spoken to in years. They had grown up in the same neighbourhood, and though they had drifted apart over time, their connection had always been warm. Aditi was now living in Delhi, working as a journalist, and she suggested they catch up over coffee.

Suraj agreed, curious to reconnect. A few days later, they met at a quaint café near India Habitat Centre. As soon as he saw her, Suraj felt a rush of familiarity. Aditi's energy was infectious—vibrant, full of life, and completely in sync with the city's rhythm. As they sat down and started talking, it felt like no time had passed.

"I've been reading your poems," Aditi said with a smile. "You've come a long way since we were kids."

Suraj smiled back. "Yeah, I guess I have. Poetry's been my way of making sense of everything."

They spent the next few hours reminiscing about their childhood, laughing about old memories, and discussing their current lives. The conversation flowed effortlessly, and Suraj found himself feeling a lightness he hadn't felt in a long time. As they walked out of the café, the sun setting behind the trees, Aditi turned to him with a playful grin. "We should do this more often."

Suraj nodded. "Definitely."

That night, as Suraj lay in bed, he thought about how far he had come. The days of heartache and loneliness felt distant, almost like a different life. He wasn't looking for love, but he felt open to whatever life had in store for him. Meeting Aditi again had reminded him of the joy of connection, of the simple pleasure of spending time with someone who made him feel alive.

Over the next few weeks, Suraj and Aditi began meeting more often. They attended poetry events together, explored different parts of Delhi, and shared countless conversations about their dreams and aspirations. Their friendship deepened, and though Suraj wasn't sure what it meant, he was content to let it evolve naturally.

One evening, after a particularly inspiring poetry session in the heart of Old Delhi, Suraj found himself writing about Aditi. It wasn't a love poem—at least, not in the traditional sense—but rather an ode to the joy of rediscovery, of finding someone who reminded him of the beauty in the world.

"The Light You Bring"

In laughter shared, in moments still,

You bring a light, a gentle thrill.

A friendship forged in simple grace,

A warmth, a smile upon my face.

Not seeking love, not chasing dreams,

Just living life in peaceful streams.

With you, the world feels bright once more,

A door to joy, an open door.

The bond between Suraj and Aditi grew stronger with each passing day, but neither of them rushed into defining it. They both valued the connection they had, and there was an unspoken understanding that whatever happened, it would unfold naturally.

One evening, as they strolled through the illuminated streets of Chandni Chowk, Aditi turned to Suraj and asked, "Do you ever think about love, or have you given up on it?"

Suraj paused, thinking for a moment. "I don't think I've given up on it," he said slowly. "I just don't feel the need to chase it anymore. I think love finds you when you're ready."

Aditi smiled softly. "I like that."

They continued walking in comfortable silence, the vibrant energy of Old Delhi surrounding them. Suraj felt a quiet contentment settle over him. Whatever was happening between him and Aditi, it felt good. It felt right.

Weeks passed, and Suraj continued to focus on his poetry, his friendships, and his personal growth. His life was full, and yet, there was a new element of warmth, something he hadn't anticipated but was grateful for.

One evening, sitting on his balcony in Greater Noida, Suraj reflected on how much had changed. His heart, once broken and raw, had healed in ways he hadn't thought possible. He had found a balance, a peace within himself that no longer depended on someone else.

"The Heart That Heals"

Once shattered, once torn apart,

Now healed, a stronger heart.

Through pain, through loss, I've found my way,

To live, to love, to face each day.

No longer bound by love's demand,

I walk alone, yet hand in hand.

For in myself, I've found the key,

To love with grace, to live freely.

The future calls, a path unknown,

But I no longer walk alone.

Suraj closed his notebook, feeling the cool night air brush against his skin. Life was unpredictable, but for the first time, he wasn't afraid of the unknown. He had learned to trust himself, to trust the journey, and to embrace whatever came next.

And as he sat there, looking out at the distant lights of the city, he knew that no matter what the future held, he was ready

27. The Blooming Connection

Winter was giving way to spring, and Delhi was awakening with the scent of fresh blossoms. The warmth of the sun felt softer now, and the city's streets were alive with colors. Suraj had come to love this time of year—the feeling of renewal and growth resonated deeply with him. It mirrored his own journey.

Suraj's connection with Aditi had continued to grow over the past few months. Their friendship had become a significant part of his life, something he looked forward to with a sense of joy and calm. There was no rush between them, no pressure to define their relationship. It was simply about being present, enjoying each other's company, and letting things evolve naturally.

One day, as they walked through the sprawling Mughal gardens at Humayun's Tomb, surrounded by the soft hues of blooming flowers, Aditi suddenly stopped and turned to Suraj.

"You know, I've been thinking," she said, her voice thoughtful. "About us."

Suraj felt his heart skip a beat, but he stayed calm. He nodded, urging her to continue.

Aditi smiled, her eyes reflecting the sunlight. "I don't know where this is going, but I know that being with you feels... right. And I don't want to lose that."

Her words hung in the air between them, filled with a gentle vulnerability that Suraj understood all too well. He had been careful with his heart, ever since Maya, but with Aditi, things felt different. There was no pain, no fear. Just a quiet understanding.

"I feel the same way," Suraj replied, his voice steady. "Whatever this is, I'm in no rush to define it. I just want to see where it goes."

They continued walking, the air between them light and full of possibility. Suraj had spent so long fearing the unknown, but now, he embraced it. He had learned that love didn't always have to come with drama and heartache—it could grow quietly, like a flower blooming in the warmth of spring.

"The Gentle Bloom"

In silence, love begins to grow,

A gentle bloom, a soft hello.

No rush, no force, just space to be,

In your presence, I feel free.

With every step, with every day,

This quiet bond, it finds its way.

No need for words to frame or bind,

For love, in time, will speak its mind.

As the days turned into weeks, Suraj and Aditi grew closer, but the ease of their relationship remained. They shared meals, explored new corners of Delhi, and often spent hours in quiet conversations, enjoying each other's company without the need for labels or expectations.

Suraj found himself reflecting on the past—how different this connection with Aditi was from his relationship with Maya. With Aditi, there was no drama, no turmoil. It was peaceful, grounded in mutual respect and understanding. It was the kind of relationship he hadn't realized he needed.

One evening, while they sat on a rooftop café overlooking the twinkling lights of the city, Aditi asked, "Do you think we'll ever define what this is?"

Suraj looked at her, taking in the warmth of her presence. He smiled. "I don't think we need to rush anything. What matters is that we're happy. The rest will come in time."

Aditi laughed softly. "You're right. I guess I've just never had something so... easy."

"Me neither," Suraj admitted. "But I think that's what makes it special."

"In Time's Embrace"

Not every love must rush or race,

Some bloom with time, in gentle grace.

In quiet moments, hearts entwine,

With patience, love becomes divine.

No need to chase, no need to claim,

For love like this, it has no name.

It simply grows, it finds its way,

And in its light, we choose to stay.

Their relationship, though still undefined, had become a source of comfort and joy for both of them. Suraj no longer felt the need to search for love—he had found something even more valuable: peace within himself, and the freedom to let love grow naturally.

Spring turned into summer, and the vibrant energy of Delhi seemed to match the blooming connection between Suraj and Aditi. They shared their poetry, explored art galleries, and often found themselves lost in conversation at small cafés scattered across the city. There was no pressure, no expectations—just a deepening connection that felt right.

One evening, after a particularly beautiful sunset at India Gate, Aditi turned to Suraj with a smile. "You know, I think we're writing our own story—one that doesn't need an ending just yet."

Suraj smiled, feeling the truth in her words. "I think you're right."

And in that moment, he realised that he wasn't just moving forward—he was truly living, embracing the present with open arms, and allowing love to find its way to him, one gentle step at a time.

"The Present Moment"

In every step, in every breath,

We find the love that knows no death.

No past to haunt, no future to chase,

Just you and I, in time's embrace.

For love is here, in now, in still,

A gentle heart, a quiet thrill.

No need for rush, no need for flight,

For love, in time, will set us right.

28. Defining the Undefined

As the monsoon season arrived in Delhi, bringing with it the scent of rain-soaked earth and the vibrant greenery that came alive in its wake, Suraj felt a shift in the air. Not just the city's changing landscape, but something within him. His relationship with Aditi had grown steadily, quietly, like the plants that thrived in the monsoon rain.

They had now been seeing each other for nearly a year. Their bond had deepened through countless moments of shared laughter, long conversations, and an unspoken understanding. Yet, despite their closeness, neither had explicitly defined their relationship. It wasn't that they avoided the conversation, but there had always been a quiet acceptance that whatever they had didn't need a label.

But one evening, as they sat in a cozy café overlooking the rain-soaked streets of Connaught Place, the topic finally came up.

Aditi swirled her cup of chai thoughtfully, her eyes watching the raindrops trickle down the window. "Suraj, have you ever wondered why we've never put a name to... us?"

Suraj looked at her, sensing that this wasn't just a casual question. "I have," he admitted. "But I've always felt that what we have is special, and I didn't want to force it into any definition."

Aditi nodded, her expression thoughtful. "I feel the same. But sometimes, I wonder if we're avoiding it because we're afraid of what it could mean."

Suraj understood what she was saying. There was a part of him that had always been hesitant to define their relationship, perhaps out of fear of repeating the mistakes of the past. But this wasn't the same as before. Aditi wasn't Maya, and their relationship wasn't built on fleeting passion or unresolved tension. It was something much deeper, much more stable.

He took a deep breath. "I think we've been hesitant because we both wanted to protect what we have. But maybe it's time to talk about it."

Aditi smiled softly. "Yeah, maybe it is."

They sat in silence for a moment, both of them absorbing the weight of the conversation. The rain continued to fall outside, creating a rhythmic background to their thoughts. Suraj felt a sense of clarity wash over him. He wasn't afraid of defining their relationship anymore because he knew it wouldn't change the core of what they shared.

"Defining Us"

In silent moments, we have grown,

A love that stands, a truth we've known.

No need for rush, no need for fear,

For love, like this, remains sincere.

But now we speak, in quiet grace,

Of what we are, the path we trace.

A bond that's true, a heart that's kind,

In love, we find the peace of mind.

Over the next few days, Suraj and Aditi continued to discuss their relationship, but the conversations weren't heavy or laden with pressure. Instead, they were light, honest, and filled with mutual respect. They both agreed that they didn't need to rush into any labels, but they also recognized the depth of their connection.

One evening, as they sat on the terrace of Aditi's apartment in South Delhi, watching the city lights twinkle in the distance, Aditi turned to Suraj with a smile.

"You know," she began, her voice soft, "I don't need a title for what we have. But I do need to know that we're moving forward together."

Suraj reached for her hand, his heart full. "We are," he assured her. "Whatever this is, wherever it goes, we're in it together."

Aditi's eyes sparkled with warmth. "That's all I need."

And in that moment, Suraj realized that love didn't need to fit into any predefined boxes. It didn't need to follow a script or adhere to societal expectations. What mattered was the connection they shared, the respect they had for each other, and the understanding that they were building something meaningful—together.

"Together in the Unknown"

In the unknown, we walk with grace,

No need for rush, no need to chase.

For in your eyes, I see my home,

No longer do I need to roam.

In every step, in every word,

Our love is felt, though never heard.

For labels fade, and titles pass,

But love like ours is built to last.

As the days turned into weeks, Suraj and Aditi continued to navigate their relationship with a sense of ease and openness. They spent weekends exploring Delhi's historical sites, visiting bookstores, and attending poetry readings together. Their bond was deepening, not because of a label, but because of the experiences they were sharing and the growth they were fostering in each other.

One day, while walking through the bustling streets of Old Delhi, Suraj felt an overwhelming sense of gratitude. He had come so far—from the heartbreak and confusion of his past to this place of peace and fulfillment. And though he didn't know what the future held, he was no longer afraid of it.

Aditi had brought a light into his life that he hadn't even realized he was missing. She had shown him that love didn't have to be complicated or painful—it could be simple, pure, and grounded in mutual respect.

That evening, as they sat together watching the sun set behind the Qutub Minar, Suraj wrote a poem for her—a tribute to the love they had found, not in the rush of passion, but in the quiet moments of companionship.

"A Love That Grows"

In every moment, we find our way,

No need for rush, no need to say.

For love, like this, it gently grows,

In hearts that trust, in peace it shows.

No fleeting spark, no burning flame,

But love that stays, that knows no name.

In every step, in every breath,

Our love will stand the test of death.

29. The Turning Point

As the summer heat settled over Delhi, Suraj and Aditi's relationship continued to blossom. They had crafted a beautiful routine, enjoying quiet evenings filled with laughter and heartfelt conversations. Yet, beneath this serene exterior, Suraj felt an undercurrent of change stirring, a whisper of uncertainty that he couldn't quite shake off.

One evening, after a romantic dinner at their favourite café, Aditi suggested they take a stroll through Lodhi Garden. The lush greenery and historical monuments provided a serene backdrop, but as they walked, Suraj noticed that Aditi seemed distracted, lost in her thoughts.

"Is everything okay?" Suraj asked, concern evident in his voice.

Aditi stopped walking and turned to him. "Suraj, can we talk about something serious?"

The weight of her tone sent a jolt of apprehension through him. "Of course. What's on your mind?"

"I've been offered an internship abroad, and I think it's a fantastic opportunity for my career," she began, her voice steady but her eyes betraying her uncertainty. "But it means I would have to leave Delhi for six months."

Suraj's heart sank. He had known Aditi was ambitious, but he hadn't anticipated this conversation. "That's amazing! You should definitely take it," he replied, forcing a smile. "But... what does that mean for us?"

"I don't want to lose what we have," Aditi said quickly, her voice rising slightly. "But I also don't want to hold you back if you're not okay with a long-distance relationship."

Suraj felt a storm of emotions swirling within him—fear, anger, and sadness. He wanted to support her dreams, but the thought of being apart was daunting. "Aditi, I don't want to hold you back either. But long-distance... it's not easy."

"Distance in Love"

Two hearts entwined, yet miles apart,

A test of faith, a fragile heart.

In whispered dreams and midnight calls,

Will love endure when distance falls?

Yet in the quiet, truth prevails,

For love is strong, though silence veils.

If hearts are true, the distance fades,

In love's embrace, all fear cascades.

As the days turned into a blur of uncertainty, Suraj found himself grappling with the decision. He spent sleepless nights contemplating what it would mean to navigate their relationship in this new reality. Each day, the anticipation of Aditi's departure loomed closer, filling him with dread.

Finally, on the eve of her departure, they found themselves back at the café where it all began. The place was buzzing with life, but all Suraj could feel was the weight of impending change.

"Aditi," he started, "I think we need to make a decision tonight."

She looked at him, her eyes glistening. "I know."

"What if we tried to make this work?" Suraj suggested, his heart pounding. "I mean, we could plan visits, call each other every day. Love can conquer distance, right?"

Aditi smiled through her tears. "I want to believe that. But I'm scared, Suraj. What if we drift apart? What if I fall in love with someone else?"

Suraj felt a pang of pain at her words. "And what if you don't? What if we grow stronger because of this?"

They spent the rest of the evening talking, pouring their hearts out, and trying to bridge the gap between their fears and hopes. They both knew the road ahead wouldn't be easy, but they also understood that love was worth fighting for.

"Together in the Fight"

In shadows deep, our fears reside,

Yet in the light, our hearts collide.

With every breath, with every tear,

Together we stand, dismissing fear.

For love is not just a fleeting spark,

But a flame that glows in the darkest dark.

So take my hand, let's face the night,

In love, we'll find our strength, our light.

30. The Reunion

Six months had passed since Aditi left for her internship. Suraj had thrown himself into his work, filling his days with poetry and painting, while also keeping the flame of their connection alive through daily calls and messages. Yet, as the months dragged on, he felt the strain of their separation.

As the end of her internship approached, Aditi suggested a reunion—a weekend in Jaipur. Suraj's heart raced with anticipation. This was it; this would be their moment to see if their love could withstand the test of time and distance.

When the day finally arrived, Suraj stood at the train station in Jaipur, his heart pounding. The moment he spotted Aditi stepping off the train, a wave of emotions washed over him. She looked different—more confident, more radiant, and yet, the same girl he had fallen in love with.

"Suraj!" she called, running toward him. They embraced tightly, and in that moment, all the months apart faded away. Over the next few days, they explored the pink city together, visiting the Hawa Mahal, Amber Fort, and enjoying local delicacies. They talked about everything—her experiences abroad, their dreams, and what the future held for both of them.

One evening, as they stood on the terrace of their hotel, overlooking the illuminated city, Aditi turned to Suraj with a smile. "I missed this. I missed us."

Suraj took a deep breath, feeling a sense of relief wash over him. "Me too. I wasn't sure if we'd be the same after all this time, but seeing you... it feels right."

Aditi looked at him, her eyes glistening. "I realised something while I was away. Love is not just about being together physically. It's about the bond we share, the understanding, the patience. It's worth waiting for."

Suraj nodded, a sense of clarity washing over him. They had both grown during their time apart, and their love had matured, transcending the limitations of distance.

"The Bonds That Bind"

Through time and space, our hearts remain,

In whispered dreams, in joy and pain.

For love is strong, it bends, it breaks,

But in the end, it always wakes.

With open hearts, we stand as one,

Two souls entwined, the journey begun.

For every tear, for every sigh,

In love's embrace, we learn to fly.

As they returned to Delhi, Suraj and Aditi decided to redefine their relationship. They spoke openly about their fears and dreams, recognizing that love was a continuous journey—a dance of understanding, respect, and unwavering support.

Months passed, and together they found a rhythm that felt right, proving to themselves and each other that love could endure. The lessons they had learned shaped their relationship into something beautiful and profound.

In time, Suraj began to write again, pouring his heart into verses that celebrated love in all its forms. His poetry reflected the journey they had taken, the challenges they had faced, and the joy they had found in each other.

"Never Give Up on Love"

Through trials faced and shadows cast,

In every moment, our love holds fast.

For in the darkness, hope will gleam,

With love as our guide, we dare to dream.

So hold on tight, dear heart, don't fear,

For love will find you, it will draw near.

In every tear, in every laugh,

Believe in love, it will lead your path.

Suraj learned that love wasn't just a fleeting moment or a passionate affair; it was a journey filled with lessons, growth, and the unwavering belief that no matter the distance or the challenges faced, love was worth fighting for. And for every broken heart, there was a chance to heal, to grow, and to love again.

As he looked at Aditi, with her laughter and spirit illuminating his life, he knew that they had built something extraordinary—a love that was resilient, deep, and unwavering.

The Beginning Within The End

Suraj closed the final page of his notebook, its once-blank sheets now brimming with the rawness of his journey—love, loss, heartbreak, and healing. The inked verses stood as a testament to the moments that had shaped him, carved him, and ultimately redefined him. It wasn't the story he had imagined for himself when he first met Parvati, but it was the story that had found him, tested him, and taught him the strength that lies in vulnerability.

Barfi, his golden retriever, was curled up at his feet, his quiet presence a reminder of the love that had carried him through the darkest nights. Suraj reached down, running his fingers through Barfi's soft fur, grateful for the unconditional companionship that had softened the ache of loneliness.

Life hadn't turned out as Suraj had planned, but it was no longer something he resented. He had learned that pain is not the enemy; it is a teacher. The heartbreak that once consumed him had given way to an unexpected strength, to a deep understanding of himself, and to a profound appreciation for the small, quiet joys in life—like the warmth of Barfi's paw on his hand, the glow of a sunrise after a sleepless night, or the soothing rhythm of his pen moving across a page.

In the months since his breakup with Parvati, Suraj had discovered a new kind of love: love for himself, love for the people who had stood by him, and love for the possibilities that lay ahead. He no longer measured his worth by the presence or absence of someone else. Instead, he found meaning in the act of creating, in the courage it took to open his heart, and in the lessons that came with every goodbye.

"The Journey Ahead"
"In every loss, a seed is sown,
From broken hearts, new roots are grown.
The scars I bear, they shine, not fade,
A map of who I am, they've made.

I'll walk this path, unknown, unplanned,
With courage born from my own hand.
The love I sought was always near,
It lived within, now crystal clear."

Suraj stood up, his notebook in one hand and Barfi's leash in the other. They stepped out into the evening, the sky painted in hues of amber and violet. The air was crisp, carrying with it a sense of renewal. As they walked together, Barfi's tail wagging with uncontainable joy, Suraj felt a quiet but profound sense of peace.

This wasn't the ending he had envisioned when he thought of love, but it was the beginning of something far greater: a life that was his own, shaped by his choices, his resilience, and his capacity to love and be loved, even in the simplest moments.

In letting go of what was, he had embraced what could be. And as the night settled around him, Suraj smiled, knowing that while the past would always be a part of him, it no longer defined him.

This was his story—a story of heartbreak, hope, and healing. A story that, in its imperfections, had become more beautiful than he could have ever imagined.

And so, with Barfi by his side and the world stretching endlessly before him, Suraj walked forward—into a future that was his to write, one step, one word, one moment at a time.

In dreams I wove a tapestry bright,
Of love and laughter, a heart's delight.
Through verses spun with hope and grace,
I longed to find my perfect place.

    Yet fate had plans, both cruel and kind,
A bittersweet dance, love intertwined.
In Parvati's eyes, I saw the sun,
But shadows whispered, a battle begun.

    The first spark ignited, a tender kiss,
In moments of bliss, pure, untainted bliss.
But doubt crept in, a thief in the night,
And soon, our love faced its darkest fight.

    With every crack, my heart would break,
Yet I held on, for love's sweet sake.
But words turned sharp, and kindness waned,
In the echoes of silence, only pain remained.

    Oh, how I poured my soul on the page,
Each line a cry, a heart in a cage.
For love once bright, now turned to grey,
In shadows of sorrow, I lost my way.

    But then came Disha, a friend in need,
Her gentle words like a nurturing seed.
Yet still, my heart bore the weight of the past,
In every smile, the shadows cast.

Through healing journeys, I learned to stand,

To embrace the pain, to understand.

For heartbreak teaches the strongest soul,

In letting go, we learn to be whole.

Then Aditi shone, a light in the dark,

In her laughter, I found a spark.

Together we wove new dreams anew,

In love's embrace, my heart broke through.

Now I pen this journey, a tale to unfold,

Of love and loss, of hearts that are bold.

For every ending is just a new start,

And love, oh love, is the truest art.

So here's to the lovers, the broken and torn,

In every ending, new love is born.

For in the dance of heart and mind,

Love's sweetest truths are what we find.